Google

Pixel 8 And 8 Pro

User Guide

**A Complete Beginners And Seniors
Picture Manual On How To Master Your
Google Pixel 8 And 8 Pro, With Step By
Step Android 14 Tips, Tricks &
Instructions**

By

John S. Trevino

professional before attempting any techniques contained herein.

By reading this document, the reader agrees that under no circumstances is the author responsible for any losses, direct or indirect, which are incurred as a result of the information contained in this book including errors, omissions, and inaccuracy.

Table of Contents

INTRODUCTION

The Pixel 8 and Pixel 8 Pro are Google's latest flagship smartphones, designed with artificial intelligence (AI) to provide a better, more tailored user experience. The Google Tensor G3 is the brains behind these revolutionary phones. Upgrades to the Android operating system, security patches, and regular feature drops will be available to them for seven years. Look at the new phones in further detail; they include improved cameras, new sensors, and a stunning design.

With its refined aesthetic, softer edges, stunning metal accents, and eco-friendly materials, the Pixel 8 and Pixel 8 Pro are perfect for daily use.

The Pixel 8, being smaller and with rounded edges, has an excellent feel when held in the palm compared to the Pixel 7. Compared to the Pixel 7, the 6.2-inch Actua display is 42% brighter, providing you with more accurate colors and details in real life. You can get the Pixel 8 in Rose, Hazel, or Obsidian, and it has a polished glass back and satin metal accents.

Pixel 8 Pro's 6.7-inch Super Actua screen is our most luminosity display to date. You will be pleasantly surprised by how accurate your Ultra HDR photos seem, even when shot in bright sunshine. It is available in three different colors— Porcelain, Bay, and Obsidian—and has a polished metal frame with a matte glass back.

Additionally, the Pixel 8 Pro's rear has a new temperature sensor that enables rapid item temperature scanning. Inspect the milk in your baby's bottle or the pan to see if it's hot enough to begin cooking. Furthermore, we have applied to the FDA to allow the Pixel Thermometer App to record your temperature and send it to Fitbit.

Additional camera enhancements

With their strong, improved camera systems, the Pixel 8 and Pixel 8 Pro capture breathtaking photos and videos. Plus, they come with editing features that will change the game.

Starting with the primary camera, all of the cameras on the Pixel 8 Pro have been enhanced to take better images and record better movies in low light. The telephoto lens shoots 10x photographs at optical quality and collects 56% more light, the larger ultrawide lens improves Macro Focus, and the front-facing camera now features autofocus for the greatest selfies on a Pixel phone.

Plus, the Pixel 8's upgraded primary camera comes with a brand-new ultrawide lens that supports Macro Focus.

You can now access your preferred picture and video modes with ease thanks to the new and user-friendly camera app. In addition, the Pixel 8 Pro comes with Pro Controls, which allow you to fine-tune the Pixel Camera's creative capabilities. These controls include things like shutter speed, ISO, and the ability to take 50 MP photographs at any magnification level, among other things.

The Camera app's Pro Controls in action.

It's happened to all of us: just when you thought you had the ideal group shot, someone starts to look away. You may acquire the snapshot you imagined taking with Best Take1 by using the photographs you took. To do this, an algorithm running on the smartphone combines many photographs to get the greatest possible appearance for each user.

A new experimental editing experience, Magic Editor in Google images employs generative AI to help you capture the spirit of the moment in your images. Subjects may be easily resized and moved with a few clicks, and you can even utilize presets to make the backdrop stand out.

If your movie contains annoying noises, such as wind noise or a large crowd, you may quickly and effectively remove them using Audio Magic Eraser1. This revolutionary computational audio feature sorts sounds into separate layers so you may regulate their volumes using sophisticated machine learning algorithms.

Video Boost, coming later this year to the Pixel 8 Pro, uses Tensor G3 in conjunction with our robust data centers to process your films at the cutting edge. It creates breathtaking, photorealistic films by adjusting brightness, contrast, saturation, stability, and graininess. For improved smartphone video quality in low light, Video Boost also activates Night Sight Video on Pixel.

Tools that enhance efficiency and productivity

More context and page depth are now at your fingertips. To help you grasp the main ideas of a site fast, Pixel has a feature called Summarize. You may listen to articles while you're on the move thanks to your Pixel's reading-aloud and website translation capabilities.2

A picture of a Pixel 8 Pro reading text from a website.

If you want to get things done more organically, you can chat with Pixel as it understands human speech subtleties even better. When you say "um" or hesitate for a moment, it will wait for you to finish before answering. Quickly compose, modify, and send messages using the sound of your voice—no matter how many languages you know.2

Additionally, Call Screen now assists you in receiving an average of 50% fewer spam calls thanks to enhanced AI.3 To engage the caller, it will secretly answer calls from unknown numbers using a voice that sounds more genuine. It can also distinguish between the calls you are interested in and those you aren't. You may soon react to basic calls, like appointment confirmations, without answering the phone by tapping on contextual answers suggested by Call Screen.

Shown on the main screen is the Call Screen.

You and your private data are safe with seven years of upgrades.

In conjunction with the Titan M2 security chip, Google Tensor G3 strengthens the Pixel's defenses against advanced threats and protects sensitive data. You can now use Google Wallet and other compatible banking and payment applications with the Pixel 8's Face Unlock, which satisfies the highest Android biometric class.

As time goes by, your Pixel phone will continue to improve thanks to the special features and upgrades you get. For the first time, the Pixel 8 and Pixel 8 Pro will get software support for seven years. This support will include operating system upgrades, security patches, and regular feature drops.4

You can pre-order the phone now and it will be available for purchase.

Starting at $699 for the Pixel 8 and $999 for the Pixel 8 Pro, you can pre-order them now. Enjoy a free Pixel Watch 2 when you pre-order the Pixel 8 Pro.5 Google Fi Wireless also offers the cheapest prices on the new Pixel phones when you pre-order them. In addition, all Pixel Watch 2 connection is included in your flexible and secure phone plan at no extra cost.

Starting on October 12, you may purchase both smartphones, together with covers designed by us and our partners, via the Google Store and our retail partners.

Details on availability and pricing for the Google Pixel 8 and Pixel 8 Pro

On a purple backdrop, a guy holds a blue Google Pixel 8.

The official announcement of the Pixel 8 and Pixel 8 Pro occurred on October 4, 2023, and its release to the public and retailers occurred on October 12, 2023. Now, the new Pixel 8 pair is accessible in a lot of markets, unlike the Google Pixel Fold. All of the following countries have access to the phones: USA, Canada, Denmark, France, Germany, Ireland, India, Italy, Japan, Norway, Portugal, Puerto Rico, Singapore, Spain, Taiwan, the UK, and the US.

This is both one of the most extensive launches for Google's mobile business to date and the most costly one in the US. The Pixel 8 is now beginning at $700 while the Pixel 8 Pro finally hits the dreaded $1,000 threshold, marking a general increase in both phones' prices. Devices across the UK and EU saw comparable price hikes; however, you should check with your local area for exact details.

Those who preorder the Pixel 8 Pro will get a Pixel Watch 2 at no cost, while those who purchase the Pixel 8 will also receive a free pair of Buds Pro. Just a few hours remain to get this offer, so if you have these gadgets in your basket, now is the time to make it happen, as we update this guide.

Also, starting two years ago, with the announcement of the Pixel 6 and Google Fi's all-in-one bundle, Pixel Pass, subscribers will no longer be able to pay for their services via the bundle. The service was discontinued on August 29th, however existing users were given a $100 credit to use on a new Pixel.

Google Pixel 8 Cameras

Pictures pixel-8-pixel-8-pro teaser 6

Talking about the Pixel series isn't complete without mentioning the camera. Impressive camera skills were the foundation upon which Google constructed its successor to the Nexus program. The company combined state-of-the-art hardware with innovative software and AI-powered picture processing. Historically, Google has been somewhat consistent with its camera sensors; the business didn't finally get rid of the one it had been using in the Pixel 3 until the release of the Pixel 6. That, however, is about to change with this year's roster.

Aside from the primary sensor, the Pixel 8 Pro has three brand-new sensors. Both phones have the same 50MP lens, which now has an f/1.68 aperture, which is rather remarkable. To no one's surprise, it can crop in to double the zoom effect, and it is still using pixel binning. Super Res Zoom, which is also available on the smaller Pixel 8, uses the same lens and has a maximum magnification of 8x.

Google Pixel 8: A Picture of Lifestyle

The Pixel 8's ultrawide remains the same, while the Pro gets a whole new sensor. An amazing 125.5-degree field-of-view is accompanied with a 48MP f/1.95 lens. Also brand new is the periscope telephoto lens, which has a 48MP sensor and an aperture of f/2.8. A digital crop of up to 30x is once again possible with the Pro thanks to Super Res Zoom.

Both versions include a 10.5MP front-facing camera with an f/2.2 aperture, but the Pro model has autofocus. Regardless, they may both enable face unlock with authentication, which is a significant improvement over the phones from last year. There is still a lot of emphasis on software. With the release of Magic Editor comes the long-awaited addition of tools to enhance your films and photographs, such as Video Boost and Best Take. With the addition of Night Sight capability, the Pixel 8 has the potential to become one of the top Android phones for low-light recording.

CHAPTER ONE

KNOW ABOUT PIXEL 8 AND PIXEL 8 PRO CALL SCREENING

Have you had enough of unsolicited calls, scams, or spam on your Google Pixel devices? Learn how to enable call screening on your Pixel 8, Pixel 8 Pro, Pixel 7 Pro, or any other Pixel smartphone with this comprehensive guide. If you want to know who's contacting you before you answer the phone, you may use the call screening option on your Google Pixel. When Google Assistant receives a call, it immediately determines who is calling and why. The caller takes the time to listen to the Assistant's responses before deciding to answer or not.

Pixel smartphones in the US only have the option to automatically filter calls. In addition, you may manually enable screen calls on Pixel devices in several countries, including Spain, Canada, Japan, the United Kingdom, Italy, France, and Germany.

Pixel8, Pixel 8 Pro, and Pixel 7 Pro Call Screening Configuration Guide

To utilize the call screen function, you must ensure that your area supports it. Google Pixel smartphones in the US only allow you to manually or automatically activate the call screen.

Google Pixel Can Screen Calls Automatically

Your Pixel devices will use call screening to identify private numbers or unknown callers.

Go into your Pixel device's phone app.

In the upper right corner, you should see three vertical dots; tap on their names.

Select the Preferences.

Go to the Call Screen and Spam menu.

Access the option to see the caller and spam ID.

Your Pixel 8 Pro's screen for spam and calls

Press the Call icon.

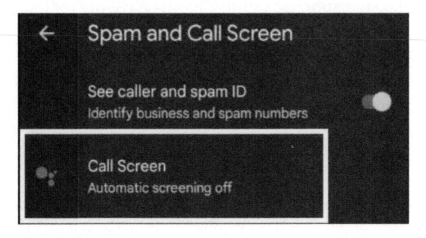

Screening Calls on the Pixel 8, Pixel 8 Pro, and Pixel 7 Pro: How to Configure

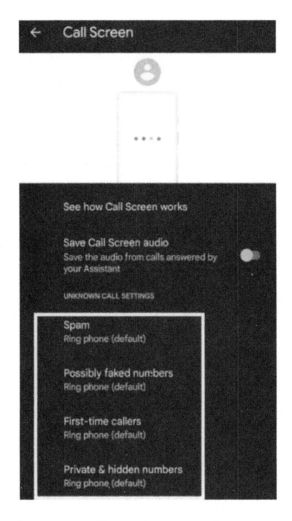

In the Unknown call settings section, tap on Spam, Possibly counterfeit numbers, First-time callers, or Private & concealed numbers. Then, pick an option.

17

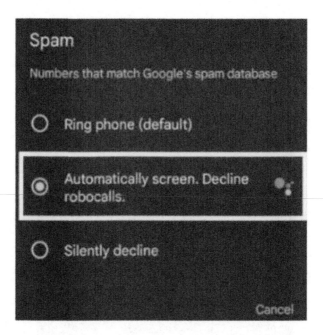

Pick an automatic screen once you click the "We Select Spam" option. Opt out of receiving robocalls.

If the Call Screen settings are not visible on your Pixel smartphone, it means that your device does not support this function.

Turn on the Google Pixel's Call Screen by Hand

Open the phone app, then go to Menu > Settings > Call screen. Just do what it says on the screen.

When your Google Pixel smartphone detects a call from an unknown number, you will be able to watch the Screen call. Google Assistant will respond by inquiring about the caller and the reason for their call. Take a look at the queries that have been recommended, such as "Report as spam," and I will return your call. Do you need my help right away? I'm confused.

How to Record Screened Calls on the Google Pixel Phone > Start > Preferences > Screen for Spam and Calls > Call screen > Click the "Save call screen audio" button.

Go to the phone app and go to the "Recent Calls" section. The number clearly shows the Google Assistant. Press on the Transcript to read the whole chat.

Press and hold the screened calls until you see the Trash symbol; then, touch on it to delete the transcript and recording.

That concludes it. How often do you filter incoming calls on your Google Pixel? Tell me which feature of the Google Pixel you love the most. Post yours in the comments area.

The latest mobile photography champion is Google's Pixel 8 Pro camera.

EXPLORING THE GOOGLE PIXEL 8 PRO'S CAMERA MODULE

The camera is the most anticipated feature of the latest Google Pixel 8 (and 8 in general) smartphones. Given Google's dominant position in computational photography, tech enthusiasts who are interested in cutting-edge photography will be closely monitoring this smartphone's annual upgrade. For some reason, I'm always curious about new camera technology because my life is a constant struggle between wanting to shoot beautiful images and wanting to travel light.

Every megapixel

During the Pixel 8 launch event, Google highlighted the phones' upgraded camera modules. All of the 8 Pro's sensors have been upgraded, including the ultrawide, which has gone from 12 to 48 megapixels. This is in addition to the 50-megapixel primary sensor and the 48-megapixel sensor used for the 5x optical zoom.

Defaulting to a 12.5-megapixel final picture, Google uses all those megapixels to do some computational wizardry, which sacrifices some detail in favor of better color rendering, noise reduction, and other features. This saves storage space and doesn't drain your battery life. However, if you want to record at the maximum resolution of the sensor, you may activate the high megapixel mode. This comes in helpful when you need to print or trim the picture, for example.

The Pixel 8 Pro captured a full 50-megapixel JPEG.

An image of a fungus growing on a wood, cropped from a 50-megapixel Pixel 8 shot.

The variety of choices available here is great since it allows you to tailor them to your requirements: Google will take care of the hard work to ensure you get a nice outcome when you shoot in JPEG with basic settings for social and friends/family sharing. Alternately, you may shoot in high megapixel mode and save the images as JPEGs, giving you more options for editing and sharing. On the other hand, you may go all out by capturing in RAW+JPEG mode and using a high megapixel. This will give you highly editable RAW files that you can then manipulate in Lightroom or any other suitable editing program. Plus, you'll have a JPEG that's ready to share and has Google's picture magic performed.

A look at the RAW and JPEG file types used by the Google Pixel 8

The Pixel 8 Pro camera shoots in RAW, which is softer and less vivid, instead of JPEG.

When shooting in JPEG with Google's autocorrection applied, the 5x zoom produces outstanding results in high-resolution mode, with plenty of information and clear rendering. If you're looking for a pocketable camera with a long-range optical zoom lens, having all that information accessible at that range is a significant plus. It also eliminates the need to carry along a separate camera body.

These photographs are also made more acceptable by the ultrawide's enhanced resolution, but it remains the camera with the lowest quality in my tests. But, with its enhanced focusing and higher resolution, it does provide some intriguing macro results (more on that later).

A preview of the ultrawide camera on the Google Pixel 8 Pro

How far can you go?

The new "Pro" options are exclusive to the Pixel 8 Pro. Testing has shown that this seems to be mostly a software-locking decision by Google. You should think about whether the Pro options will be helpful to your workflow and needs, considering what they provide, regardless of why they're only available on the 8 Pro.

Instead of letting Google decide depending on the scenario, lighting, etc., you can change the resolution from 12 MP to full 50 MP, shoot in RAW+JPEG, and choose manually between three hardware lenses.

The camera settings panel of the Google Pixel 8 Pro

Although there isn't much, these options are essential for getting the most out of your editing software photographs, so it's little wonder Google adds the "Pro" label. Most confusing, in my experience, was the lens selection setting, which caused the camera app to crash (which was fixed in an update that went out the same day the review embargo was lifted) and also made it possible to override Google's software smarts, which could lead to lower overall image quality if you made the wrong choice.

Although these features seem arbitrarily reserved for the Pro model, they are highly helpful and are located in a separate tab under the camera app's main settings menu. I get that it's a differentiation, but I'm crossing my fingers that Google will eventually let non-pro Pixel 8 devices have them.

Macromania

With the new ultrawide camera's improved resolution and focusing, Google made a big deal out of the Pixel 8 Pro's improved macro capabilities. In reality, I discovered that macro mode is capable of achieving some very remarkable outcomes; but, it is still not as failsafe as, say, the main camera.

Photo with the Google Pixel 8 Pro, this macro photo shows the underside of a mushroom.

The Google Pixel 8 Pro captured this macro image of a mushroom's underside.

Taking handheld macro photographs outside in less-than-ideal lighting conditions is the most common source of difficulty. Other common obstacles include wind and shade. While the computational photography feature of Google does a great job of reducing camera shaking, I found that even when getting very near to the subject, the final shot still had a hint of blur. Not to mention how difficult it is to zero down on the focus precisely.

Google Pixel 8 Pro macro image of a leaf

Snapped this close-up of a leaf with the Google Pixel 8 Pro.

Having said that, the subsequent macro images are still quite impressive, ideal for digital and social media usage, and a significant improvement over previous generations.

The conclusion

Thanks to its camera system that works out of the box to an extent that few of its competitors can even try to match, Google receives huge accolades. Photos taken with this front-facing camera have an exceptional quality that is unmatched by any other smartphone camera system. The color rendering, sharpness, blurring in portrait mode, dynamic range, and pretty much everything else contribute to this. Does it still not hold a candle to a high-end fixed-lens camera or a specialized one with interchangeable lenses? Certainly, but for the average person who isn't shooting images for publication or business, the difference is becoming more irrelevant. The Pixel 8 Pro is unrivaled by any other smartphone if a good camera is your top concern.

PHONE APPS FOR THE PIXEL 8 AND 8 PRO THAT RECORD CALLS

Users have high expectations for the Google Pixel 8 series because of its stellar reputation for software features. The Pixel 8 Pro goes above and above with its Pro improvements, building upon the software advances offered by the Pixel 8. On the other hand, many people wonder whether the Google Pixel 8 and 8 Pro can record phone conversations. Here, we'll take a look at the many ways these devices may record calls, and then suggest several great applications for the job.

Call Recording on the Google Pixel 8 and 8 Pro: Is It Possible?

Unlike earlier Pixel devices, the Pixel 8 series does not come with the ability to record calls automatically. Nevertheless, these smartphones may be equipped with third-party programs that enable call recording. Let's go over the available features for each device separately.

Are Google Pixel 8 calls recordable?

Sadly, the Pixel 8 lacks a built-in capability to record incoming calls. Nevertheless, with the help of third-party call recording applications, your Google Pixel 8 may still record calls. In addition to recording calls in good quality, these applications include a ton of other useful functions. Let's take a look at a few top-rated Pixel 8 call recording applications.

1. Yeezy

Among the many useful features offered by eyeZy, a trustworthy call recording software, are extensive parental control options. In addition to recording incoming calls, it can also record departing calls with excellent quality. You can keep tabs on several apps, including social media, using eyeZy's activity tracker. The app's built-in GPS tracker allows you to zero in on the precise whereabouts of the desired gadget. With support for both iOS and Android, eyeZy offers a flexible option for recording calls on the Pixel 8.

2. The guru

With the help of the VoIP software Keku, users may make cheap domestic and international calls. Keku is a VoIP service that also has a call recording option. You may record crystal-clear calls with the Keku Call Recorder and keep them in your app for up to 30 days. With an upgraded membership, you may upload recordings for up to three months, and then download and share them with whomever you choose. Keku is an app that you can download for free on your Android or iOS smartphone. Some of its features, however, do need a subscription.

3. The Cube ACR Call Recorder

One specialized call recording program, Cube ACR, is well-known for its ability to integrate with a wide range of third-party apps, including Skype and WhatsApp. You may choose between automatic and manual call recording in the app. Even better, you may set up automated call recording for certain contacts. Cube ACR may be downloaded for free, but to use the backup function, you'll need to subscribe. Cloud storage options, such as Dropbox and Google Drive, are available to subscribers who want to save their recordings online.

4. Via Google

You may already be acquainted with Google Voice if you're a Google Pixel 8 user. Even though it's mostly a voice-over IP service, Google Voice lets you record your calls. Unfortunately, you can't use this function unless you pay for one of their programs. With the $20 Standard plan, you can record calls whenever you like, and with the $30 Premier plan, you can record calls automatically. Google Voice is compatible with other Google Workspaces and has several additional capabilities.

5. PhoneApp

If your company needs VoIP software for all of your phone calls, OpenPhone is a great choice. You may easily record both incoming and outgoing calls using its call recording capability. Additional capabilities, such as the ability to share recordings with team members and auto-generated call transcriptions, become available to customers when they upgrade to the Business plan. With OpenPhone, you may enjoy the freedom and convenience of using it on your PC, Android, or iOS device.

Will the Google Pixel 8 Pro be Able to Record Phone Calls?

The Pixel 8 Pro cannot record calls using either the built-in or third-party applications, in contrast to the Pixel 8. On purpose, Google has disabled any way for the Pixel 8 Pro to record phone calls. Owning a Pixel 8 Pro will therefore render all call-recording applications unavailable to you. This restriction is an intentional design choice that sets the Pixel 8 Pro apart from other Google Pro models.

In summary

Finally, there are third-party programs that can record calls, even if it isn't built into the Google Pixel 8 series. Apps like as OpenPhone, Google Voice, eyeZy, Keku, and Cube ACR provide dependable call recording alternatives for Google Pixel 8 users. Unfortunately, recording calls is not an option on the Google Pixel 8 Pro due to Google's restrictions on the device. You can make sure that the recordings made on your Google Pixel 8 are of great quality by utilizing the applications that are suggested.

THE BATTERY LIFE OF THE GOOGLE PIXEL 8 PRO

The 5,050mAh battery within the Pixel 8 Pro is an exact 1% increase in nominal capacity compared to the power pack seen in the previous iteration. The Pixel 8 Pro, except for the minor non-upgrade, is similarly equipped to other top-tier Android handsets.

Compared to the Galaxy S23 Ultra and the iPhone 15 Pro Max, the phone's Active Use scores aren't very impressive. In particular, the iPhone's statistics are much higher. Plus, there's no guarantee that it will last longer than the little Pixel 8.

Rate of charging

The Pixels' charging speed is one area that hasn't gotten much praise—or, more accurately, we've been griping about how sluggish they charge every time. The findings we obtained from the Pixel 8 Pro are a good start, but they won't change the game.

Examining the Google Pixel 8 Pro

Full charge time from flat to 1:23 hours on the Pixel 8 Pro, a gain of over half an hour over the admittedly glacial Pixel 7 Pro, was measured using Google's official 30W charger (though any decent current USB Power Delivery brick rated for that or above should do just fine). Although the Galaxy S23 Ultra's one-hour time isn't exactly lightning fast, it's still far better than the iPhone 15 Pro Max's sluggish performance. Also, after the 30-minute point, we can tell that the Pixel is doing better than the previous generation, but it isn't quite competing.

Wireless charging for the Pixel 8 Pro can reach 23W when using the official Pixel Stand, or 12W when using third-party Qi-compliant pads that meet the requirements of the Extended Power Profile standard. For whatever reason, the Wireless Power Consortium's database does not yet include any certified Pixel 8 phones.

CHAPTER TWO

HOW TO TURN OFF YOUR PIXEL 8 PRO OR 8

To disable the Pixel 8 Pro or Pixel 8, follow these steps. If you want to conserve power on your Google Pixel 8 series, turning it off will turn off the screen, all processes, applications, and networks. Turning on your Pixel smartphone will restore all of your stored data and update the operating system.

Turning Off Your Google Pixel 8 or Pixel 8 XL

The following techniques may be used to manually turn off a Google Pixel 8 series device.

1. Launch the Quick Settings Panel and press the Power Button.

How to Use the New Power Button in Quick Panel to Power Down Your Pixel 8 Pro or 8

Two swipes down from the top of the quick panel will bring up the Power button symbol; touch on it.

The Google Pixel 8 and the Pixel 8 Pro should be turned off.

You may turn off your Pixel smartphone by tapping the Power off option in the power menu.

2. Power Button: To power off the Pixel 8, long-press the power key. This will bring up the power menu, from which you can choose Power off.

3. Use the Power and Volume Up keys To access the power menu, long-press the power and volume up keys until you see Power off.

4. Using the Accessibility Menu, Disable Google Pixel 8

Locate Accessibility in the Settings app and press on it.

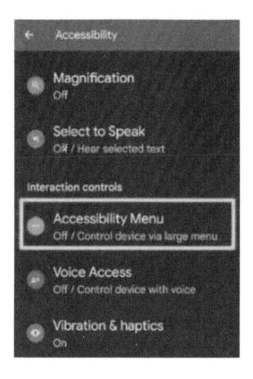

You may disable your Google Pixel phone's accessibility features in the Settings menu.

Find the section on interaction controls and scroll down to the Accessibility menu. Tap on it.

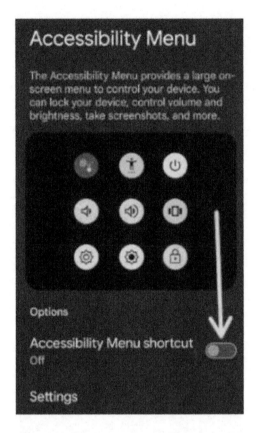

Press the Allow button once you've toggled on the Accessibility Menu shortcut to disable Pixel 8 Pro.

On a Pixel 8 smartphone, enter the accessibility menu by tapping the Accessibility button.

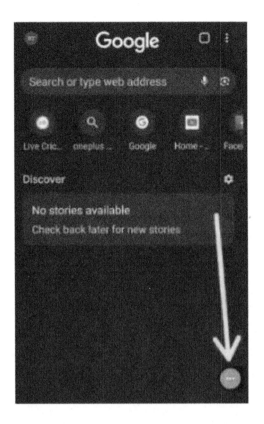

Press the Accessibility icon on the screen of your Pixel.

To reach the power menu on your Pixel 8 series, tap the Power button in the accessibility menu.

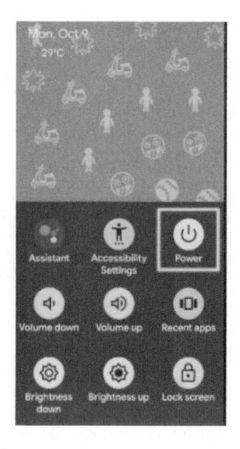

To access the power menu on your Google Pixel 8, press the Power icon. To turn off the Pixel 8 series, hit Power off.

5. Utilize the Gmail Assistant

Disable your Pixel Phone with the Help of Google Assistant

To turn off your Google Pixel, open the Google Assistant by saying "Hey Google." Then, choose the option to "Power off" your device.

The screen displays the power menu. To power down your Pixel smartphone, tap the Power button.

SET UP YOUR GOOGLE PIXEL 8'S ELECTRONIC SIM

The eSIM is compatible with the Google Pixel 8 and 8 Pro. But unlike the time-tested way of inserting a physical SIM card into your phone, activating your eSIM requires some effort. Even while Pixel phones have supported eSIM for a long time, there hasn't been much progress in making the user experience better. Whether you're upgrading from an older Pixel phone or just want to know how to activate an eSIM on your Pixel 8, this article has you covered.

These procedures are compatible with the three main US carriers as well as with smaller carriers' less expensive data plans. If you're sick of using your eSIM on Pixel, you may transfer it to any other Android phone, even the most budget-friendly ones.

The components need to activate an eSIM

With the eSIM compatibility of the Google Pixel 8 and Pixel 8 Pro, all that's needed is the device. Where to purchase this updated version of the classic SIM card can be a mystery to those who aren't acquainted with it.

All you have to do to activate your Pixel 8 with an eSIM is hook it up to a Wi-Fi network—something we'll get into later on.

Your carrier should give you a QR code with your eSIM to the email address linked to your account if you already own a Pixel 8. Get in touch with your service provider beforehand if you are missing this QR code.

The Google Pixel 8 eSim activation process

While setting up your Google Pixel 8, activate your eSim. Resetting your Pixel 8 is not necessary in the event that you choose to activate it at a later time or encounter a problem. When you're ready to activate your eSim, follow the on-screen prompts.

During setup, activate an eSim.

Just after you connect your phone to Wi-Fi, your carrier's network will ask you to join if you purchased an item with the phone. It usually takes about five minutes to get an eSIM profile using this method.

You may manually locate your eSIM by following the procedures below if it does not appear at this point.

After you've set up your phone, activate an eSim.

Whether you are new to the Pixel 8 or simply making the move, this approach can activate an eSIM at any moment. Just be sure you have the QR code that your carrier has supplied on hand. If you are unable to locate a QR code, please contact the customer care department of your carrier.

By using the camera app on your Pixel phone to scan the QR code, you may bypass most of these processes. The box that confirms the download will load after this.

1. Launch the Settings app on your Pixel 8.
2. Hit the Network and Internet button.
3. Access SIM cards.

Image captured from the settings menu of an Android 14 Pixel phone

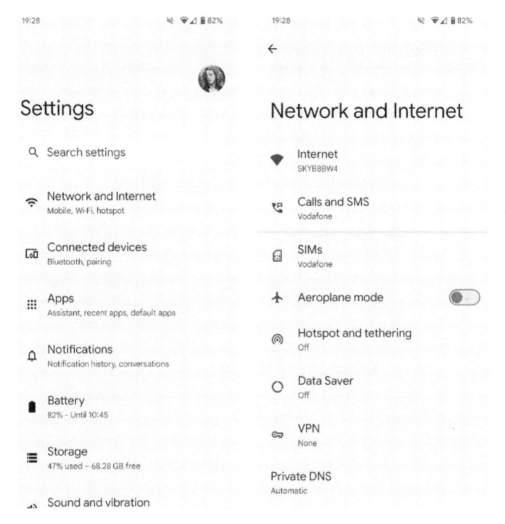

Image taken from the network and internet settings menu of an Android 14 Pixel phone

4. Press the "Add SIM" button.
5. Tap Get a fresh eSIM card.

Image taken from the esim download screen on an Android 14 Pixel phone

Image of the SIM card tray on an Android 14 Pixel phone

6. Take a look at the QR code that came with your phone plan.

Image captured from the scan esim window on an Android 14 Pixel phone

7. To verify your eSIM, go to the bottom right of your screen and press on Download.

The download of your eSIM will take around five minutes. Your Pixel phone will connect to your carrier's network immediately after the download is complete.

Simple steps to transfer an old eSIM to your new Google Pixel 8

Transferring your eSIM straight from an earlier Pixel phone to a newer Pixel 8 or Pixel 8 Pro eliminates the need to manually deactivate and reactivate it. Even though the Pixel 8 is the only Pixel phone that supports eSIM transfers, any Pixel phone that supports eSIM transfers may be used.

When you're setting up your brand-new Pixel 8 phone, this option will show up.

Deactivate the eSIM on your previous phone and then activate a new one once you've set up your Pixel 8. You may have to contact your service provider for this.

Displayed on a canvas blanket, a Google Pixel 8 Pro smartphone rests next to a verdant pumpkin.

Get your Pixel 8 ready to use an eSIM with a regular SIM card

Follow these instructions to activate an eSIM in your Pixel 8 if it already has a SIM card installed. Because of this, it is possible to use a single phone with two SIM cards.

Most carriers allow you to use an eSIM in conjunction with a SIM card or another eSIM. Nevertheless, this feature could be limited by some carriers. Alternatively, you may save many eSIM profiles and then utilize just one of them.

Am I able to activate my eSIM with any carrier?

Yes. Though the process differs from phone to phone and carrier to carrier, eSIM activation is becoming more widely available. In case the procedures mentioned above don't activate an eSIM on any of the three main US carriers (Verizon, T-Mobile, and AT&T), you may refer to our tutorial.

Talk to your service provider if you're still confused. They may either remotely activate it or show you how to do it. To get your eSIM activated and downloaded, you may have to go to a physical location of your carrier.

Use your Pixel 8 to stay in touch

The Tensor G3 processor in the Pixel 8 mostly resolved the connection problems that plagued the Pixel 6 and Pixel 7. When used with an eSIM, it prevents you from accidentally disconnecting from the network.

Although this was enhanced in the Pixel 8, it came with a few issues when it was released. To get over these problems, you may do a few simple things.

HOW TO INSERT AND REMOVE A SIM CARD

If you're experiencing activation difficulties, errors, a blank or frozen screen, or trouble connecting to your browser, following the instructions on inserting or deleting your SIM may help.

While your Pixel 8 or 8 Pro is turned on, do not try to insert or remove the SIM card. You risk damaging your smartphone or SIM card if you do this.

1. Make sure the gadget is not turned on.
2. To remove the card tray, start at the bottom left corner of the device (with the display facing up) and put the SIM removal tool into the hole.

The tray will eject once you push in.

Please use the SIM removal tool.

3. Choose from these:
   - Put the SIM card in.

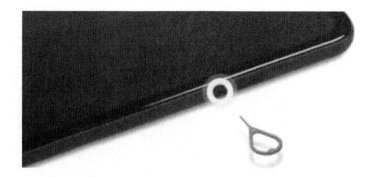

With the gold contacts facing up, place the SIM card into the tray using the notch on the card as a guide.

Place SIM

- Taking the SIM card out

Pick up the card from its holder.

Sim animation removal

4. Return the tray to its original place in the phone's slot by carefully pushing it back in.

CHAPTER THREE

HOW TO CONFIGURE YOUR GOOGLE PIXEL

Advanced Google Pixel 8

If you're like most people, you can't wait to get your hands on the shiny new Google Pixel 8 Pro and see what all the fuss is about. To get the most out of your smartphone, however, there are a few basic settings you should adjust before you dive headfirst into the app and widget ecosystem. Get the most out of your Pixel 8 Pro by following this 10-point checklist.

1. Give Each Device Its Distinct Name

A distinctive name for your Pixel 8 Pro should be your first order of business. Find "Settings > About Phone > Device Name" in your phone's menu and give it a meaningful name. In addition to adding a unique touch, this will help other devices, such as Bluetooth speakers or laptops, recognize your device when you connect it.

2. Find the Best Range for Your Battery

One of the most important features of any smartphone is its battery life. Press the "Adaptive

Charging" button in the "Settings > Battery" menu. Your phone's battery life will be increased, allowing it to stay functioning for a longer duration, thanks to this. Additionally, you have the option to show the battery % on the status bar and execute battery diagnostics.

3. Use AI Wallpapers to Your Advantage

One special feature of the Pixel 8 Pro is the ability to personalize AI-generated backgrounds. Find the AI wallpaper option in the wallpaper settings and touch on it. After that, you may make the wallpaper your own by tapping on the highlighted text to alter its aspects.

4. Decide on a Navigational Approach

Both gesture and three-button navigation modes are available on the Pixel 8 Pro. Navigate to "Settings > Display" and choose the option that suits you best. To further cater to your navigational preferences, each mode also has supplementary customization choices.

5. Get Good at Hand Signals

Several gestures have been included in your Pixel 8 Pro to provide a more natural and fluid user experience. Navigate to "Settings > System >

Gestures" to activate or disable these features. Here you may access functions that come in quite helpful in different scenarios, such as one-handed mode or the flip-to-mute option.

6. Adjust the Camera's Parameters

The camera is a notable feature of the Pixel 8 Pro. Learn how to use the manual controls for settings like focus, shutter speed, and ISO to get the most out of it. You may also activate grid lines for improved picture composition and vary between 12 and 50 megapixel resolution.

7. Modify the Settings for Video Recording

The Pixel 8 Pro is an excellent choice for those who like taking videos. You have the option to record in either 1080p or 4K inside the camera app. If you want smoother or more detailed video, you may change the frames per second.

8. Personalize the Quick-Shot Function

Quick facts like the current date and weather are available via the home screen's At-a-Glance function. You have the option to turn it off if you find it annoying. On the other hand, you may personalize it to display just the data that is relevant to your needs.

Summary

Although the Google Pixel 8 Pro has a ton of functionality, you have to go into the settings menu to find out what it can do. If you want to get the most out of your gadget, whether you're just starting or want to use it for a long time, these first adjustments are essential. Yes, you can take your Pixel 8 Pro experience to the next level by making these tweaks.

CHARGING AND BATTERY LIFE OF THE GOOGLE PIXEL

The long-awaited release of the Pixel 8 series, Google's next flagship phone, has happened. A plethora of intriguing new Google goods were unveiled during the October 4th, 2023, Made by Google event. Except the Pixels, aren't we?

If you're wondering about the Pixel 8's battery life or charging capabilities, we've got you covered in today's post. Countless surveys on PhoneArena have shown the critical importance of battery life; hence, it is time to discover the Pixels' composition in milliampere hours.

Is the Pixel 8's battery life superior?

When it comes to the Pixel 8's battery life, there are two main considerations. Firstly, the battery capacity of the Pixel 8 family was somewhat increased compared to the previous generation.

Next, the Pixel 8's state-of-the-art Tensor G3 chipset. We anticipate some respectable improvements in efficiency, and by extension, battery life, from the next Tensor and Pixel 8 handsets, considering the efficiency difference between the first and second versions of this chipset. Below you can see the results of our tests conducted on the Pixel 8 smartphones. Everyone who loves Pixel, rejoice!

The above graph amply demonstrates that the Tensor G3 chipset outperforms its predecessor. By around an hour and a half, the Pixel 8 Pro surpasses the last model in terms of web surfing performance, and by about the same amount, in terms of video streaming. When compared to its predecessor, the Pixel 8 offers half an hour more time for YouTube watching and 1.5 hours more for surfing the web.

We need to retake the tests to be completely sure, but we obtained some disgusting findings, so the gaming issue is now somewhat contentious. So, to get the whole story, stay tuned. When compared to their predecessors, the new Pixels have greater battery life.

For the Pixel 8, what is the battery life?

The battery capacity of the Pixel 8 series was somewhat enhanced. View the table that follows.

Google Pixel 8 Pro	10h 32 min
Google Pixel 7 Pro	9h 39 min
Google Pixel 8	9h 36 min
Google Pixel 7	9h 13 min

Google Pixel 8 Pro	15h 51 min
Google Pixel 7 Pro	14h 19 min
Google Pixel 8	15h 39 min
Google Pixel 7	13h 56 min

Google Pixel 8 Pro	6h 42 min
Google Pixel 7 Pro	4h 11
Google Pixel 8	6h 33 min

There is a little rise in capacity to 5,050mAh on the Pixel 8 Pro, up from the 4,926mAh on the Pixel 7 Pro, and a marginal increase in size to 4,575mAh on the Google Pixel 8 model, representing a 5% gain over the previous generation.

	Pixel 8	Pixel 8 Pro	Pixel 7	P
Battery capacity	4,575 mAh	5,050 mAh	4,270 mAh	4
Wired charging	24W	27W	20W	
Wireless charging	18W (with Pixel Stand 2nd gen)	23W (with Pixel Stand 2nd gen)	12W	

Can the Pixel 8 be charged wirelessly?

There's an upside to it. Both the Pixel 8 and the Pixel 8 Pro can charge wirelessly. With the 2nd generation Pixel Stand, your Pixel 8 can get up to 18W of wireless power, while the Pixel 8 Pro can receive up to 23W of wireless charging assistance, according to Google. Both devices may be charged at 12W using any other Qi-certified wireless charger.

Can the Pixel 8 be charged wirelessly in reverse?

Yet another affirmative response. Support for reverse wireless charging is included in the Pixel 8 series. This function is referred to as Battery Share by Google. The Pixel 8's battery life will naturally reduce due to this feature's design for charging Qi-certified devices. The charging speeds for the Battery Share function are not disclosed by Google; instead, the company only says, "Charging speeds may vary." Having said that, your Pixel can be used to charge a variety of wireless devices.

Which charger is compatible with the Pixel 8?

The Pixel 8 series may be charged using a USB-C cable, which supports rates of up to 30W (albeit it isn't included with the device). If you own a Pixel 8 and want to charge it quicker, you may get a Pixel Stand or use a Qi-certified wireless charger, both of which support wireless charging rates of up to 12W. Here are a few of the finest chargers for Pixels that you can find.

How quickly can the Pixel 8 be charged?

The new Pixel 8 and 8 Pro both saw a 4W increase in their wired charging speeds, going from 20W to 24W and 23W to 27W, respectively. Until the Pixel 8 phones arrive at our test lab, we won't know whether the increased power will result in quicker charging speeds. However, in principle, we should see somewhat faster charging on the new Pixels.

In summary

That concludes it. All the information we have on the charging and battery life of the recently revealed Pixel 8 and Pixel 8 Pro smartphones. The page has been updated with the initial benchmarks, however to get consistent results, we will need to rerun the gameplay test. Keep watching. However, at this time, the Pixel 8 family outperforms the previous generation in terms of battery life. Yey!

CAN YOU CHARGE YOUR GOOGLE PIXEL 8 WIRELESSLY?

The Pixel 8 has wireless charging, so let's go over everything.

Back of the Google Pixel 8: Rose 4.

Now that the Google Pixel 8 series has been announced, we are aware that many of you are considering purchasing one. Before you buy, there are a lot of things to think about; our review of the Pixel 8 and Pixel 8 Pro will go into more detail on these topics. Wireless charging is a determining factor for a lot of people. Can you charge your Google Pixel 8 wirelessly?

Can you charge your Google Pixel 8 wirelessly?

Phase 2 of the Google Pixel Stand

Wireless charging is an option for both the Google Pixel 8 and the Pixel 8 Pro, as stated in the previous brief response; however, there are a few key distinctions to bear in mind. The benefit of the doubt goes to the Pixel 8 Pro, thanks to its 23W wireless charging capability. When using wireless charging, the regular Pixel 8 can only achieve rates of up to 18W.

Wow, that's very quick! However, a second-generation Google Pixel Stand—which retails for $79 on Amazon—is required to achieve such rates. The charger's built-in fan makes it suitable for use with higher wireless charging rates.

You can only use up to 12W when using other conventional Qi wireless chargers. Because of this, the Google Pixel Stand is, without a doubt, the greatest wireless charger for the Pixel 8 series. However, if you're interested in exploring other possibilities, we also have a list of the top wireless chargers generally.

Will the Google Pixel 8 be able to charge itself wirelessly in reverse?

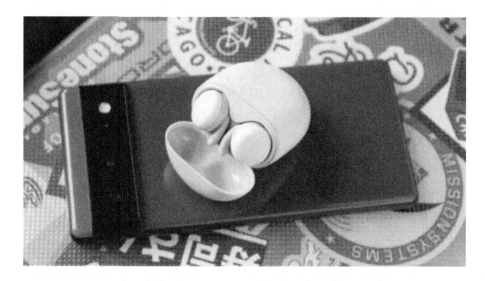

Using a Pixel 6 smartphone with the A-Series earphones from Google.

Reverse wireless charging is an option for the Google Pixel 8 and Pixel 8 Pro, thus the answer is yes. So, you may use the phone to charge other gadgets and devices wirelessly. Use it to power up your smartwatch or true wireless earphones, for instance. Keep in mind that you cannot utilize Power Share with the Pixel Watch 2 since it does not enable wireless charging.

If you own a Pixel 8 series phone and want to charge additional devices, you'll need to activate a function called Battery Share.

A Google Pixel phone's Battery Share feature:

1. Get the Settings app started.
2. Change to Battery.
3. Select "Battery Share" from the menu.
4. Switch to using battery sharing.

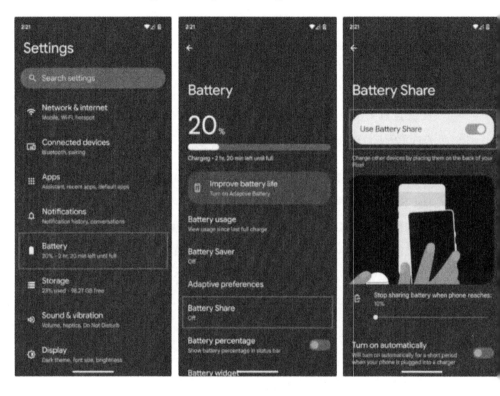

How to Turn on Battery Share on a Google Pixel Phone (1) - Is Wireless Charging Available on the Pixel 8?

CHAPTER FOUR

HOW TO TRANSFER DATA TO PIXEL IS SIMPLER

All the sales and the holidays are quickly approaching. If you or a loved one are considering getting a Google Pixel 7 or Pixel 7 Pro as a holiday present but are put off by the thought of migrating from iOS to Android, I'm pleased to tell you that the procedure is rather simple.

Your chosen data, including contacts, images, and messages, will be transferred over when you link your previous phone with your Pixel 7. And it usually only takes about half an hour to complete! We have summarized four ways that switching is now simpler than ever before for people who are making the transfer.

Transferring data is as simple as connecting, choosing, and transferring.

With the included USB adaptor, you can easily transfer all of your data from your old iPhone to your new Pixel. After you've connected, the Pixel screen will show you what to do to complete the transfer.

Do not lose any of your messages, contacts, or other information.

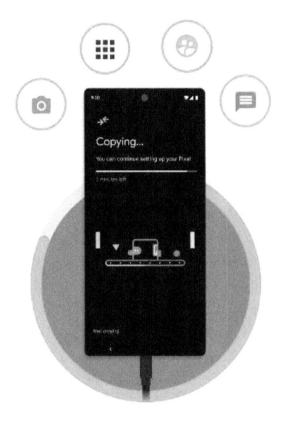

You won't have to give up your favorite applications, old messages, and phone connections just because you're a part of Team Pixel. Screen prompts will walk you through the process of transferring data from your iOS smartphone to your Android device after you connect the two phones via a cable. This will include:

- Persons to Contact
- Images and footage
- Texting, multimedia, and iMessage services
- Calendars, music, and iCloud storage
- Record of phone calls
- Notes
- Plus much more; our Help Center has all the details.

Using Google Photos on your new Pixel to peruse your picture library of loved ones—both human and animal—will make you forget you ever left your previous phone. Unless you're using a Pixel, in which case you can fix blurry photographs from an older phone using Photo Unblur and eliminate distractions from otherwise great shots with Magic Eraser.

Moving photographs from iCloud

What on earth is that? Are you saying that you have backed up all of your images to iCloud and not to your actual phone? No problem at all; Google is also useful for this.

You may begin transferring photos from iCloud Photos to Google Photos at privacy.apple.com even before you get your Pixel smartphone. With Google One, you get 15 GB of storage, which is three times more than what you may be accustomed to. However, if you still find that it's not enough, you can expand your plan here.

How does iMessage work?

Any other iOS or Android device can communicate with your Pixel. On top of that, we're doing everything in our power to enhance cross-platform messaging for both Android and iOS, including implementing response support and more. To prevent iMessage from reading your messages, we advise that you remove your number from the service when you upgrade.

With that out of the way, you may confidently buy a Pixel 7 for yourself or someone else, since any individual can join Team Pixel after connecting, selecting, and transferring. And the best part is that the Pixel 7 has so many useful AI-powered experiences already installed. This includes a top-notch camera, rock-solid security, and exclusive Pixel features like Call Screen, Direct My Call, and Hold For Me. For more information on these features, check out this link.

METHODS FOR MOVING INFORMATION FROM AN IPHONE TO A PIXEL

If you follow the on-screen instructions during setup, transferring data from your old iPhone to the Pixel is a breeze. But if you don't complete the setup the first time or if you forget a step in transferring the data:

After seeing the message "Pixel setup isn't done," you will be prompted to "Finish setup."

- After a few days, go to Settings and choose Finish setup from the menu at the top of the screen if the setup is still not complete.
- Resetting your device may be necessary if it has been some time. Nevertheless, your data files will be permanently erased.
- After you've set up your Pixel device, here are two tried-and-true ways to move your data from your iPhone to it.

A simple way to move data from an iPhone to a Pixel

Part one focuses on using a third-party tool called MobileTrans - Phone Transfer to transfer data from an iPhone to a Pixel. If you own many smartphone models, including Android and iOS, this software is a godsend for transferring data between them. A few of the functions of MobileTrans-Phone Transfer are as follows:

Quickly transfer media from iPhone to Android, including photos, videos, calendars, messages, contacts, and audio files.

- Media files from popular Android phones may be easily transferred to the new iPhone 15.
- System requirements for iOS 17 and Android 13 are fully met.
- Big Four, Sprint, Verizon, and T-Mobile are just a few of the well-known carriers that this software is compatible with.
- Putting the features aside, here are the three easy methods to transfer your iPhone data to Pixel.

Start by launching MobileTrans once you've installed it.

Get the desktop version of MobileTrans from the developer's website and run the setup file. Launch the app and go to the main window. From there, choose Phone Transfer.

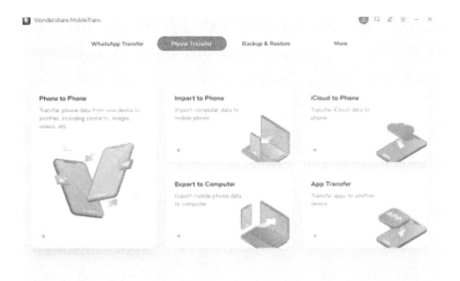

WhatsApp Transfer   Phone Transfer   Backup & Restore   More

Phone to Phone
Transfer phone data from one device to another, including contacts, images, videos, etc.

Import to Phone
Import computer data to mobile phone

iCloud to Phone
Transfer iCloud data to phone

Export to Computer
Export mobile phone data to computer

App Transfer
Transfer apps to another device

MobileTrans residence

After that, connect your iPhone or Pixel to your computer using the USB cords. In the Source phone field, enter iPhone. In the Destination phone field, enter Pixel. To help you with this choice, there is a Flip button.

Decide which files you want to transfer to your new Google Pixel.

Two, find the information you want to transfer to the Pixel phone in the list that appears on the right side of your iPhone. Mark the box next to the text that says "Clear data before copy" if you want to remove all of the current data on Pixel. Otherwise, press the Start button without checking the box.

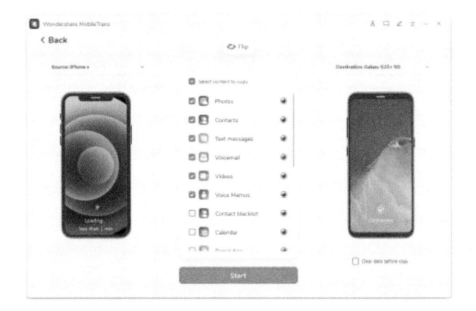

Picking the files to transfer and then pasting them into Pixel

Pixel Preview

The whole duration of the data transmission to Pixel is proportional to the size of the chosen data. Once that is done, you can verify that all of the data was successfully moved to the Pixel phone.

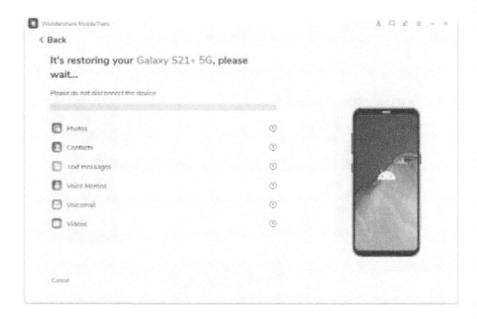

Examine the replicated files

There you have it! Data migration from iPhone to Google Pixel is now complete with a single click.

This article explains how to use the Quick Switch Adapter to move data from an iPhone to a Pixel. It becomes more intriguing as you scroll down.

Use the Quick Switch Adapter to Move Data Between Your iPhone and Pixel

This alternative approach is long and rather specific. To move information from an iPhone to a Google Pixel if MobileTrans is unable to do the job, please refer to the instructions provided below. I recommend reading it twice: once before you begin the transfer, and again as you go along, since there are a lot of procedures to follow and it's easy to forget anything.

Make sure all of the files you stored on your Pixel phone are accurate.

After the setup is complete, we will take care of the data transfer from your iPhone to Pixel. Therefore, the files that were not transferred during setup are the ones that need to be moved to the new Pixel.

Be ready to move data files.

Before you transfer data from your iPhone to Pixel, there are a few things you need to clarify. Here are:

1. Prior to beginning the transfer, ensure that both phones are either completely charged or linked to a stable power source.
2. Ensure that you own the Quick Switch Adapter, as well as your SIM card, and the necessary equipment to install it, as well as functional iPhone USB cords.
3. Turn off iMessage on your previous iPhone. This is particularly important if your iPhone is in the possession of a school or company, since they will likely obstruct the transfer procedure.

4. After you've inserted the SIM card into your Pixel phone, turn it on. On the screen of the phone, you'll see a Start button.

Go ahead and move your info from your iPhone to your Google Pixel.

1. On a Google Pixel phone, press and hold the Start button. The next step is to link the phone to a reliable mobile data or Wi-Fi network. Paste your data into the designated area.
2. The next step is to turn on the iPhone and then input the passcode.
3. Next, connect the iPhone and the Quick Switch Adapter using their corresponding USB wires. After that, snugly attach the Pixel phone to the Quick Switch Adapter. Kindly follow this specific sequence to complete the connection.
4. Next, sign in to your Google account on your Google Pixel after tapping on Trust on your iPhone. Proceed with the steps to establish a new Google account if you do not already have one.
5. Your phone's screen will now display a list of all data files. If you want to copy all the files, go ahead and click Copy. In any case, before you hit transfer, make sure all the data you want to transfer to Pixel is unchecked. Go to the Apps section and remove the ones you aren't interested

in. Just because you can easily find Android versions of iPhone applications doesn't mean you should replicate them.

6. A list of all the transferred files will be sent to you when the transfer is complete.

Data transfer from an iPhone to a Pixel using a Quick Switch Adapter may seem daunting at first glance, but it's really rather simple once you get the hang of it. Similar to MobileTrans-Phone Transfer, there are three steps to the process otherwise.

What follows is a table that compares the two ways that data may be transferred from an iPhone to a Google Pixel.

Evaluate the Two Approaches

MobileTrans - Phone Transfer allows you to transfer data from your iPhone to your Pixel. Data transfer from iPhone to Pixel using Quick Switch Adapter

- Data files may be transferred more easily when phones are linked to computers.
- The transmission may take place even when phones aren't linked to Wi-Fi or cellular data networks.
- Downloading and installing the MobileTrans app is a must to use it on any given device.

- It is not possible to send some types of data files without purchasing a business license from the app.
- The phones don't need to be fully charged prior to the transfer.
- The Quick Switch Adapter allows users to transfer data files from their phones.
- During the transfer procedure, phones must be connected to Wi-Fi or a mobile data network.
- The transfer tool is easily accessible, so there's no need to download or install anything.
- You may send as many different sorts of files as you like.
- Make sure the phones are fully charged before the transfer so they don't abruptly shut off.

Here are the main distinctions between the two methods—Quick Switch Adapter and MobileTrans—for transferring data from an iPhone to a Pixel. In this manner, you can easily figure out which approach is ideal for you.

Nonetheless, the two methods work well for moving the most common data file types and applications. In terms of effectiveness, they are just as simple to use.

RESETTING A GOOGLE PIXEL TO FACTORY SETTINGS

Before you can do a factory reset, it's wise to back up your data and remember your Google account credentials. This way, you'll always have access to your stored data, regardless of whether you end up using the same phone again or obtain a new one. Read our piece titled "How to set up automatic backups for your Google Pixel, and save an unlimited amount of photos and videos." if you want to know how to back up your Google Pixel.

To avoid losing power midway through the resetting process—which might take up to an hour—you should also connect your phone to its charger.

Here is how to factory reset your Pixel when you're ready:

1. Access the Settings app by swiping down from the top of the screen and tapping the gear symbol.

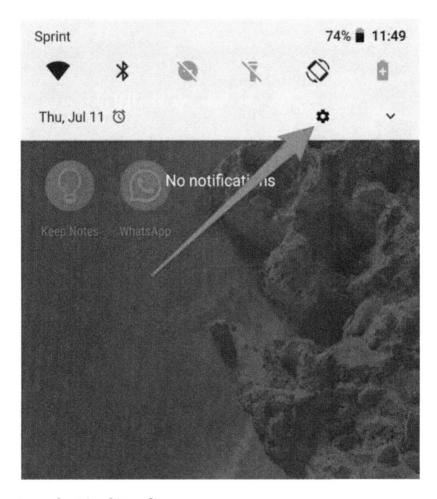

Google Pixel Backup

Press the gear icon to access Settings.

2. Hit "System" followed by "Reset options."

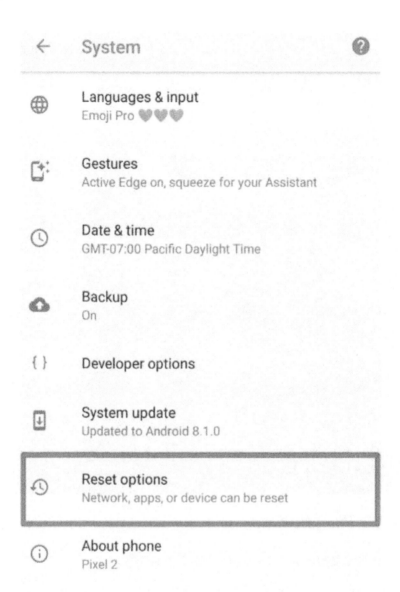

Google Pixel Factor Reset

Find the Reset options menu and click on it.

3. After selecting "Erase all data (factory reset)" from the menu, tap "Reset Phone" (you may be prompted to input your PIN, password, or pattern to verify this).

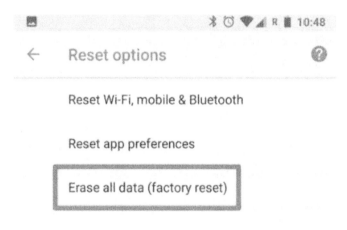

Google Pixel Factor Reset

To begin the factory reset, tap "Erase all data" and then confirm.

4. Use the "Erase everything" option to reset your Pixel to its original factory.

Methods for resetting a Google Pixel to factory settings

Once you've finished resetting your phone, you'll have to restart it and then use your Google account credentials to recover the data that was saved up.

That may be accomplished by connecting to Wi-Fi and then restarting the device according to the on-screen prompts. Click "Next" once you reach the "Copy apps and data" box, and then choose "Can't use old phone."

Following that, choose "Ok" under "Copy another way," and finally, "A backup from the Cloud." After you've followed the rest of the steps, you may return to your Google account and retrieve the data that was backed up.

CHAPTER FIVE

HOW TO COMMUNICATE VIA YOUR PIXEL PHONE

The Phone app, along with other widgets and applications that display your contacts, allows you to make phone calls.

The majority of the time, you can touch on phone numbers to call them. In certain versions of Google Chrome, you may copy the number to the dial pad by tapping on the highlighted part.

Get the Phone app from the Google Play Store if you don't already have it.

- Your smartphone may not be compatible with the Phone app if you are unable to download it.
- To make the app your default app after downloading it, just follow the on-screen instructions.

You'll need Android 7.0 or later to complete any of these tasks.

Call someone

The Phone app will not work until you accept the request to make it your default.

1. Get the Phone app on your mobile device.
2. Choose a contact:
   - Press the Dial pad Keypad to input a number.
   - Press on Contacts Contacts to choose a stored contact. Based on your call log, we may

provide you with recommended contacts to call.

- Press Recents Recent to choose from a list of numbers you've phoned lately.
- Press the Favourites Speed dial button to choose a contact from your Favorites list.

3. Hit the "Call phone" button.
4. Press the End call button after the call is over. Dragging the call bubble to the bottom right of the screen will restore your call if it has been minimized.

Video calls, video conferences, and RTT calls are also possible with certain operators and devices.

Respond to or decline a call

Your screen will display the caller's number, name, or caller ID information whenever you get a call. Verified will appear above the caller's name or number when Google is able to verify a phone number.

- In a locked phone, you may either touch Answer or slide the white circle to the top of the screen to answer the call.
- When your phone is locked, you may reject the call by swiping the white circle to the bottom of

the screen or by tapping Dismiss. Callers who are not accepted may still leave a message.

- Simply swipe up from the Message symbol and choose New message to quickly reject the call and send a text message to the caller.

Tips:

- You have to put the call you're on hold for to answer another one.
- You may use your voice to answer or refuse calls if you have Google Assistant enabled. You may ask Google to answer a call by saying so.
- Tell Google to ignore the call.

Opt for phone call features

During the course of a call:

- Press the dial pad keypad to open the keypad.
- Tap Speaker Speaker to toggle between the earpiece, speakerphone, and any Bluetooth headset that is attached.
- Choose Mute Mute to toggle the microphone on and off.
- Pressing Hold Hold will stop the call without disconnecting the caller. Once you've tapped Hold, you may take up the call again.

- Press the Switch Switch button to toggle between the active calls. We will put all other callers on hold.
- By selecting "Call merge," you may combine all of your active calls into a single event. Please merge.
- Select "Home" from the menu to dismiss the call.
- Simply drag the call bubble to reposition it.
- Use the 'Hide' button at the screen's bottom to conceal the call bubble.

There are operators and gadgets that allow you to:

Opt for a video chat instead: Press the video call button Chat via video.

1. Changing the recipient of an ongoing call:
2. Tap on Add call Add when a call is in progress.
3. Type in a contact number.
4. Hit the "Call phone" button.
5. Once the call is connected, press the Transfer button. After you input your number in Step 2, your call will be sent to that number.

HOW TO ACTIVATE THE CLEAR CALLING FEATURE

The Clear Calling feature is not on by default on the Google Pixel; here's how to enable it.

Using Clear Calling might help when background noise becomes too much to handle. Despite the feature's importance, it is not activated by default on the Pixel. In this tutorial, we'll show you how to activate it and explain why you should.

Explain Clear Calling.

Clear calling could seem like a simple way to improve the quality of your own voice-over phone conversations at first look. That idea is really backward.

Pixel smartphones include an app called Clear Calling that can automatically muffle the other party's background noise. Another perk of clear calling is that it makes the other person's voice sound better on your Pixel.

Due to the challenges posed by the minimal cellular coverage required for even the most basic phone calls, clear calling requires either Wi-Fi or a good mobile network connection in order to function. A stable network or Wi-Fi connection is essential for the laborious process of removing ambient noise and amplifying a single audio stream.

Instructions for Enabling Clear Calling

Since clear calling relies on an internet connection, it's probable that Google would prefer not to secretly charge consumers for their network fees. Users with limited data may be liable for the price if clear calling is enabled by default.

Regardless, you should definitely activate and leave enabled the functionality. To activate clear calling, you'll need a Pixel 7 (or later, including the 7a), since it is a function that was added to the Pixel series of devices very recently.

1. Proceed to the Pixel's settings.
2. Find "Sound and vibration" and touch on it.
3. Locate Clear Calling and activate it by tapping on it.

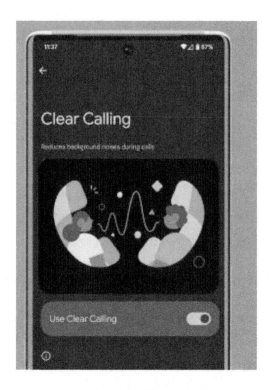

When the opposite party is experiencing a great deal of background noise during your conversation, you may find that clear calling improves the quality of your encounter. You have the option to disable it and enable it just for calls that need data saving. As an additional note, we are unsure of the data consumption associated with clear calling, although it is probably lower than that of streaming video.

Extra features that may have slipped your mind

When we deactivated clear calling, we also deactivated a few additional calling capabilities. For example, both Hold For Me and Google's automated Call Screen are turned off by default. Both are part of Google Assistant's repertoire of abilities and have the potential to streamline the phone call experience.

Any time a call comes in, you'll notice an option to use Call Screen. Before you respond, it will take over and show you who's calling and what they want. An excellent feature, although disabled by default, is the ability to make it do so automatically for unknown numbers. Even with the latest Pixel, Hold For Me remains unchanged. The function effectively mutes a company's hold music and restores audio when a live person answers the call.

HOW TO INITIATE VIDEO CALLS ON A GOOGLE PIXEL 8 PRO

Use your Google Pixel 8 Pro to make video calls. It's great for keeping in contact with faraway loved ones, holding virtual meetings at work (thanks to the rise of telework), staying in touch with coworkers while sick, and even meeting virtually before meeting in person.

The 6.7-inch LTPO OLED screen on the Google Pixel 8 Pro can accommodate video calls with ease, due to its 120Hz, HDR10+, 1600 nits (HBM), 2400 nits (peak), 108.7 cm2 (~87.4% screen-to-body ratio), resolution of 1344 x 2992 pixels, 20:9 aspect ratio, and 489 pixels per inch density.

Click the link and follow the instructions if you also want to record the videoconference you're about to have with your Google Pixel 8 Pro. You may use it for evidence, memories, or to share it with others. Google Pixel 8 Pro screen recording

Android devices, like the Google Pixel 8 Pro, don't come with a built-in video calling app like Apple devices do. Instead, you'll need to install third-party apps. If your Google Pixel 8 Pro already has some of these apps installed, great! If not, you'll just need to download and install them. Trust me, it's super easy and takes no time at all.

If you own a Google Pixel 8 Pro with 128 GB of internal memory and 12 GB of RAM, 256 GB of internal memory and 12 GB of RAM, 512 GB of internal memory and 12 GB of RAM, or 1TB of internal memory and 12 GB of RAM, you can use any of these apps to make high-quality group video calls or individual video chats. Plus, all of these apps are free, so you can use them on your mobile phone or tablet without spending a dime:

Video chatting by Skype

After being bought by Microsoft in 2011, Skype became the oldest video conferencing program in the world. It is presently supported by the operating system and most devices. Use your Pixel 8 Pro with Google's latest operating system, Android 14.

Skype: how can I get it?

Go to the "Play Store" on your Google Pixel 8 Pro, type in "Skype," hit "Install," and then hit "Open" after the installation is finished. In case you don't already have one, you can easily create one on your Pixel 8 Pro screen by hitting the corresponding link. You'll need an account with either Microsoft or Skype. "Don't have a user profile? Make one.

You may also use Skype on a desktop computer, laptop, or other device running Windows, Mac OS X, Linux, or via a web browser. You can even use it on a device with Amazon Alexa or an Xbox gaming console.

Online Meeting with Google

Google Meet can be found in the "Play Store" on your Google Pixel 8 Pro. To install it, open the app, then select "Install." After the installation is finished, you may open the app. In order to use it on your Android 14, you'll need a Google account. If you don't already have a Google account, you can easily establish one in a matter of minutes; otherwise, you'll need to log in right away without any issues.

Online Meeting with Google

To start a video chat on your Pixel 8 Pro, launch Meet. When prompted, grant Meet access to your Google contacts as well as the ability to use your camera and microphone. You may choose to deny the request for location access if it asks. Your Google Pixel 8 Pro includes GPS, GLONASS, GALILEO, and QZSS, so you won't need to give it to make a video call. To proceed with the video call and contact other people, you'll need to provide your phone number. Google Meet will send you a confirmation code by SMS, which you must input.

The interface is straightforward but could be a bit intimidating at first. To initiate a call, enter the contact's name or phone number into the search bar. If you don't see it, it means they don't have the Google Meet app installed. In this case, you can send them an invitation by clicking the "Invite friends" button.

Creating a group video call is the first step. Go to the home screen, click on "Create group," and then choose the group. After that, hit "start" to begin the call.

Adding participants to an ongoing video conversation is not feasible once it has begun; instead, you will need to establish the group beforehand.

The ability to make video chats from almost any device with a camera, microphone, and internet connection is one of Meet's many features. Thanks to its compatibility with iOS and Android devices as well as its website, the Pixel 8 Pro can be accessed from a variety of devices, including smart displays like the Google Nest Hub Max, and a wide range of wireless networks, including 802.11 a/b/g/n/ac/6e/7, tri-band, and Wi-Fi Direct.

Snap chat

With this app, you can do more than just add filters to your videos and photos; you can also use your Google Pixel 8 Pro's selfie camera (10.5 MP, f/2.2, 20mm ultrawide), 1/3.1", 1.22μm, PDAF) to make video calls to your Snapchat contacts. Just a friendly reminder that the person you wish to make a video call with needs Snapchat as well, not only an account but also to be friends on the social network.

Launch a discussion with the individual you want to speak with by tapping the chat icon on your Google Pixel 8 Pro's top right corner.

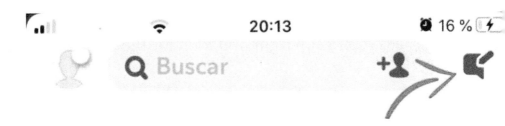

Then press the video camera icon in the upper right to start the video call.

Then, to begin the video call, click the camera icon in the top right.

Instagram

If you own a Google Pixel 8 Pro and want to use its 10.5 MP, f/2.2, 20mm (ultrawide), 1/3.1", 1.22μm, PDAF selfie camera for video calls with your Instagram contacts, you can do it through this Facebook app. Just remember that the person you want to call needs Instagram as well, so they need to have an account and be friends on Facebook.

To initiate a discussion with a specific user, just go to the screen's top right and look for the chat icon.

Then press the video camera icon in the upper right to start the video call.

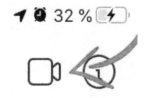

Photosharing app Instagram

Then, to begin the video call, click the camera icon in the top right.

Because of its immense popularity and the fact that almost everyone has a WhatsApp account, WhatsApp is presently the most utilized app for making video calls to friends and family.

Before you come back here, make sure you have WhatsApp installed on your Google Pixel 8 Pro. If you haven't already, visit the link to see the steps.

In order to initiate a video call on WhatsApp with a Pixel 8 Pro, whether it's for two people or a group, you'll need to locate the contact in your phonebook, open a chat with them, and then locate the video camera icon in the top right corner of the screen. Pressing this icon will start the call.

Using WhatsApp for video calls

After a video conference has begun, you may invite other people to join by tapping the plus sign (+) in the top right corner of the Pixel 8 Pro screen, and then searching for the person you want to invite.

You can also create a video call for every member of an existing group by clicking the phone symbol in the top right and choosing "video call." This will initiate a video call to every contact in that group.

You have the option to select between the Pixel 8 Pro's front and rear cameras in WhatsApp video calls. The front camera has 10.5 MP, f/2.2, 20mm (ultrawide), 1/3.1", 1.22μm, PDAF, and the rear camera has 50 MP, f/1.7, 25mm (wide), 1/1.31", 1.2μm, multi-directional PDAF, multi-zone Laser AF, OIS, 48 MP, f/2.8, 113mm (telephoto), 1/2.55", 0.7μm, dual pixel PDAF, OIS, 5x optical zoom, 48 MP, f/2.0, 126^s (ultrawide), 0.8μm, and dual pixel PDAF.

IMO

It's possible to use the free app imo on your Google Pixel 8 Pro running Android 14 as well as on desktops and laptops running Windows XP, Vista, 7, 8, or 10 as well as on Android devices, Apple iPhones, and iPads.

Messenger on Facebook

As a hidden feature of Facebook Messenger, you may also use your Google Pixel 8 Pro to conduct video calls inside this Facebook app.

To initiate a video call, choose a contact and then hit the camera icon in the top right.

Online Video Chat on Facebook

FaceTime

While the Google Pixel 8 Pro does not support initiating video calls, it does support joining group conversations and receiving FaceTime video calls.

On a Pixel 8 Pro, how can I join a FaceTime call?

Video conferencing requires an Apple device user to initiate the connection and then provide you the FaceTime link via email or text. To access the video conference, you'll need to click the provided link, provide your name, and finally, click the "Join" button.

CONNECT A WI-FI NETWORK TO YOUR GOOGLE PIXEL

Join a Public Wi-Fi Network

1. Swipe up from the Home screen to see all the applications.
2. Find the icon for Settings. Network & internet.
3. Verify that the On icon (Wi-Fi switch, top right) is switched on.
4. Select the desired network by tapping on it in the Wi-Fi networks section.
5. You may manually add the desired network if it isn't already there.
6. When asked, input the correct password and then hit the Connect button.
7. When prompted, you may see the password being typed by tapping the Show password button.
8. Click on Advanced options if you need to adjust any other settings (such as proxy or IP addresses) to your liking.

Several tasks need Wi-Fi network information. Contact your ISP or the network administrator if you need help.

1. Swipe up from the Home screen to see all the applications.
2. Access the Settings menu by clicking the gear symbol and then selecting Network and Internet.
3. Verify that the On icon (Wi-Fi switch, top right) is switched on.

4. Select the "Add network" option.
5. To see it, you may have to scroll all the way down.
6. Navigate to the Network name (SSID) box and input the correct name.
7. Select the "Security field" from the menu that appears. From the right-hand side menu, choose a security setting:

No improvement made Options include: Open, WEP, WPA/WPA2-Personal, WPA3/WPA2-Enterprise, and WPA3-Personal.

Enterprise-grade WPA3 with 192-bit

To activate any further settings, such as proxy settings or IP settings, etc., tap on the Advanced options menu.

After entering the correct password in the Password area, hit the Save button.

Press the Show password button to see the password being typed.

CHAPTER SIX

HOW TO SHARE INTERNET ACCESS
Advanced Google Pixel 8

When it comes to practical smartphone features, the Google Pixel 8 Pro has you covered. Specifically, it enables methods for sharing your Internet connection. In situations when a network connection is not readily accessible, such as when a friend's smartphone lacks 4G or when your computer's Wi-Fi is not functioning properly, this feature enables you to establish a network connection. Finding out how to share the Internet on the Google Pixel 8 Pro is the last remaining task.

Key Considerations

Focusing on other features will help us to prevent misconceptions before moving to the techniques of utilizing the function. The Google Pixel 8 Pro, like other smartphones running the latest version of Android, has the ability to share the internet. It works on the concept that other devices may utilize the phone as a router, as it can be used as a Wi-Fi access point.

The Google Pixel 8 Pro requires a 3G or 4G mobile data connection with Wi-Fi deactivated in order for the option to work. Since mobile carriers are free to impose any limitations they see fit, this is still insufficient. One group that won't be able to share the load is those with unlimited data plans. Plans with a restricted gigabyte bundle are usually the only ones that can use the feature. Nevertheless, you may verify this information with your operator.

Sharing Methods on the Internet

If your cell provider hasn't put limits on it, the Google Pixel 8 Pro's ability to connect additional devices to the network will operate without any cost at all. Many different things can be done with it.

Through wireless

How the vast majority of people who possess Google Pixel 8 Pros utilize it. You have to do the following to share a Wi-Fi connection:

1. Find the settings on your device.
2. Select "Mobile Hotspot and Tethering" from the "Connections" menu (the exact name may change from firmware version to firmware version).

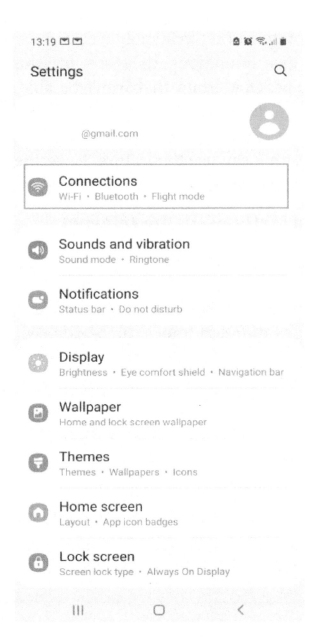

Settings

@gmail.com

Connections
Wi-Fi · Bluetooth · Flight mode

Sounds and vibration
Sound mode · Ringtone

Notifications
Status bar · Do not disturb

Display
Brightness · Eye comfort shield · Navigation bar

Wallpaper
Home and lock screen wallpaper

Themes
Themes · Wallpapers · Icons

Home screen
Layout · App icon badges

Lock screen
Screen lock type · Always On Display

Toggle the feature on.

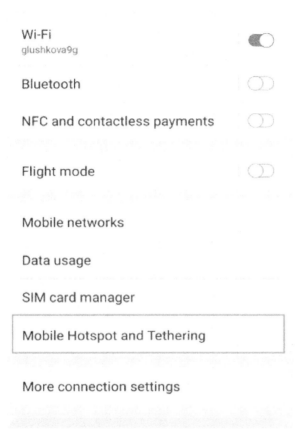

Wi-Fi
glushkova9g

Bluetooth

NFC and contactless payments

Flight mode

Mobile networks

Data usage

SIM card manager

Mobile Hotspot and Tethering

More connection settings

After that, turn on Wi-Fi on the device you want to connect to the access point, and then choose the Google Pixel 8 Pro network from the list.

Utilizing Bluetooth

While this approach is quite similar to the last one, it uses Bluetooth instead of Wi-Fi to share the network. Nevertheless, wireless connectivity is inherent to the Internet. After you finish steps 1-3 of the previous technique, you may enable the "Bluetooth tethering" slider or place a checkmark next to it to establish a connection.

Bluetooth must be enabled and the Google Pixel 8 Pro must be connected from the list of accessible networks for a device to receive communications.

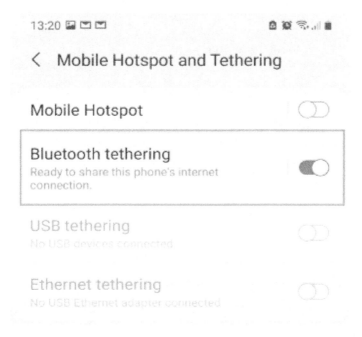

Over a USB cable

A great alternative to wireless Wi-Fi for computers that don't support it, allowing users to share their Internet connection. In this scenario, data is sent across a USB cord in its entirety:

In the settings of your phone, enable USB tethering.

1. Link your gadget to your computer.
2. Verify that the "USB tethering" mode is selected on the screen of the smartphone.
3. Go to your computer's network settings, find the new connection, and turn it on.

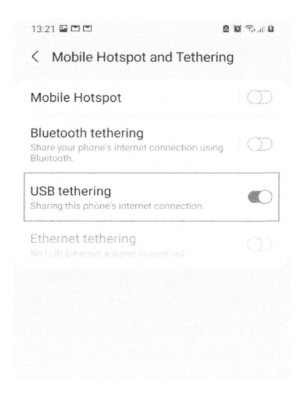

Without using a wireless Wi-Fi network, the Google Pixel 8 Pro may now transfer terabytes of mobile data to your PC. The connection may be terminated at any moment by going into the device's settings or simply removing the USB cord.

By use of a mobile app

If the in-built tools aren't cutting it for traffic distribution, consider a dedicated program like FoxFi. Similar functionality is offered on the Google Play store. Simply launch the app, enter a password, and then choose the "Activate Wi-Fi Hotspot" option to activate the access point.

You may use any other application that is comparable if needed. Google Pixel 8 Pro owners will have access to all features, including the ability to connect by USB or Bluetooth, regardless of the situation.

ACTIVATE GOOGLE'S DATA ROAMING ON THE PIXEL 8 PRO

Google Pixel 8 Pro: How to Enable Data Roaming? On what version of the Google Pixel 8 Pro can I enable data roaming? On a GOOGLE Pixel 8 Pro, how can I disable data roaming? The GOOGLE Pixel 8 Pro: How to Enable Data Roaming? On a GOOGLE Pixel 8 Pro, how can one enable data roaming?

Here we will give you the rundown on how to enable Data Roaming on the GOOGLE Pixel 8 Pro. If you're often on the go but still want to remain connected, this guide will show you how to effortlessly enable data roaming on your GOOGLE smartphone under the mobile data settings. Read the instructions carefully to learn how to enable and disable Data Roaming. If you own a GOOGLE smartphone, you should check out our HardReset.info YouTube channel.

Learn how to enable data roaming on your GOOGLE Pixel 8 Pro.

1. You should begin by opening the Settings app.

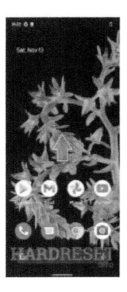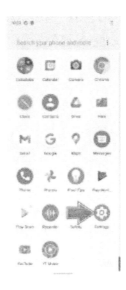

2. Get the factory reset for your Google Pixel 8 Pro.
   Motorola Moto Z Ultra Hard Reset

3. Proceed to the Network & Internet section, and
   then choose SIMs.

4. Pixel 8 Pro Master Reset by GoogleDeactivate the
Google Pixel 8 Pro's screen lock feature

Roaming mode may be activated by clicking on the switcher. Clear all data on your GOOGLE Pixel 8 Pro

5. Click the OK button to finish. Google Pixel 8 Pro Format
6. Impressive work.

Back up your GOOGLE Pixel 8 Pro

Bluetooth

Control the Bluetooth settings, check for nearby devices, connect to them, and even disconnect from a linked device.

What follows is a detailed guide on how to:

- Activate or deactivate Bluetooth in a flash • Pair with a device • Remove a device from a pairing
- When Bluetooth is not in use, switch it off to save battery life. For further details on how to connect, go to the page on pairing Bluetooth accessories.

Efficiently toggle Bluetooth on and off

To access the Bluetooth settings, swipe down from the notification bar and tap the Bluetooth symbol. From there, you may toggle Bluetooth on or off.

1. Toggle the Bluetooth on or off. To access the settings, use two fingers to swipe down from the notification bar and then tap the icon.
2. Go to Devices > Connection Settings > Bluetooth. You may toggle Bluetooth on and off using the switch.

Join forces with your gadget

1. To begin, go to the Bluetooth interface and choose Pair new device.
2. Your gadget will start looking for other gadgets on its own. Pick out the gadget you like. When asked to suggest a pairing, choose Pair.

A passcode may be requested of you; the most frequent default is 0000.

Disassemble a gadget

1. Next to the device you want to change, you should see a settings icon; click on it. This will take you to the "Connected devices" panel.

2. After that, unpair the device by selecting Forget. To confirm, choose Forget device.

If you're experiencing problems with connecting or disconnecting your device from your car, see the handbook for your specific model for further instructions.

DISCOVER THE KEY TO UNLOCKING YOUR GOOGLE

I can't remember the pattern, password, or PIN for my Google Pixel. If the fingerprint scanner is configured, you are free to utilize it. If it doesn't work, you'll have to either attempt unlocking the software or restore your Pixel to factory settings.

Once the device has been factory reset, you will be able to change the PIN and use the backup to recover your images, contacts, and other data. Tell me what to do.

A small number of Pixel users have experienced device lockouts. Although some Pixel 2 and Pixel 3 users have experienced the same problem, the majority of reports have been about the Pixel XL and this flaw. A factory reset has been Google's only fix up to this point.

Use Google's Find My Device to do a factory reset.

If you want to reset your Pixel quickly and easily, then you should turn it on, make sure it's connected to the internet, and activate Location and Find My Device. The ability to reset your PIN from another device is no longer available via Google Find My Device; a factory reset is now your sole option.

1. Access Google Use the computer, tablet, or other device to access Find My Device.
2. Verify that Google has found the right phone.
3. Get rid of

We can remotely delete all data from your Google Pixel. Upon completion, you will be able to set it up similarly to a new phone, generate a new PIN, and restore an earlier backup.

Use recovery mode to do a factory reset

Using the hardware on your phone, you may do a factory reset on your Pixel using this approach.

If you get a "no command" warning when executing the operation, you must press and hold the POWER button, then press and hold the VOLUME UP button, and then release the POWER button.

1. Put your Pixel phone to sleep.
2. To enter Fastboot Mode or see the Android logo, press and hold the power and volume down keys simultaneously.
3. Once you've hovered over RECOVERY MODE using the VOLUME buttons, you may choose it with the POWER button.
4. Select "Wipe Data/Factory Reset" using the volume controls, and then hit the power button.
5. Press the power and volume buttons to confirm your choice.
6. When it's done, choose REBOOT SYSTEM. RIGHT NOW

You are now able to restore a backup and set up your phone with a new PIN.

Utilizing software to unlock pixel

Try using Pixel lock screen removal software if you're concerned about losing important data and photographs without a backup. You may find alternatives that promise to circumvent your lock screen without affecting your data, such as iMyFone LockWiper.

Before you give any third-party software a go, be sure it passes muster. Not only do some of them cost money, but they may also try to implant spyware on your phone. Keep in mind that there is no assurance that unlocking software won't delete all of your data, so you should probably just do a factory reset before using it.

Instructions on how to secure your Google Pixel phone with fingerprint authentication and erase your fingerprint data if necessary.

FINGERPRINT SCANNER FOR THE GOOGLE PIXEL

The fingerprint scanner on the Google Pixel may aid with data security.

- If you have a Google Pixel phone, you may skip entering passwords and usernames altogether by linking your fingerprint sensor.

- By logging into your account using the Pixel's fingerprint scanner, you may authenticate in-app purchases via the Google Play Store.
- You have considerable leeway in how you unlock your Pixel since it may store many fingerprints simultaneously.
- The fingerprint reader may also be used to wake up and unlock your Pixel.

The fingerprint sensor in the Google Pixel is multipurpose; it can unlock the phone, open accounts protected by a password manager, and even make payments.

It doesn't take long to add fingerprint security to your phone. Tell me what to do.

A guide on adding a fingerprint scanner to the Google Pixel

1. Tap the gear icon to access your settings.
2. Choose "Security & location."

🔍   Search settings

 **Network & internet**
Wi-Fi, mobile, data usage, hotspot

Connected devices
Bluetooth, driving mode

Apps & notifications
Permissions, default apps

Battery
58% - Should last until about 1:00 PM

Display
Wallpaper, sleep, font size

Sound
Volume, vibration, Do Not Disturb

Storage
48% used - 33.38 GB free

Security & location
Play Protect, screen lock, fingerprint

Accounts
Google, Adobe, Messenger Lite

Access the Security menu on your device.

3. Select "Pixel imprint" to see the fingerprint options.

4. to proceed, you may be asked to provide your PIN or password. You will be asked to establish a PIN or password before proceeding if you do not already have one.
5. To add your fingerprint(s), follow the setup process that appears on the screen. Repeated tapping of the fingerprint sensor will save your print. Adding a fingerprint (or more) to your smartphone is a breeze with the help of the wizard.

Lift, then touch again

Keep lifting your finger to add the different parts
of your fingerprint

Lift finger, then touch sensor again

Biometric Sensor

6. Pressing the sensor many times will allow it to scan your fingerprint completely. Business Insider (Michelle Greenlee)

You may continue to add more fingerprints to your device once you have uploaded one. If you harm a finger, Google suggests including a minimum of five.

7. Hit "Done" once you're done adding fingerprints.

Fingerprint authentication on a Google Pixel: the ropes

You may unlock your phone by tapping and holding your finger on its fingerprint reader located on the rear. Before you can use the fingerprint reader to unlock certain models, you may have to hit the power button.

Unfortunately, not all applications are compatible with fingerprint unlock/login. When the feature becomes available, you will be asked to log in using your fingerprint. When you use your fingerprint to log in, apps will not keep a record of it.

when it's used to log in.

9:02 99° •••⦙ 🕐 ⊙ ▼◢ 🔋57%

Fingerprint added

When you see this icon, use your fingerprint for
identification or to approve purchases

You may be required to scan your fingerprint to access some applications.

A Google Pixel user's guide to fingerprint management

Any time you want, you may disable fingerprint authentication.

To remove a fingerprint from Pixel Imprint, just touch the bin symbol that appears next to it. You won't have to input your fingerprint anymore; your secondary unlock method will take over.

Essentials of The Fingerprint Security

Though it's handier, fingerprint login isn't as safe as other login methods like PINs or passwords. One example is the possibility of using a fingerprint scan to unlock your phone.

In addition to fingerprint unlock, the Google Pixel has other security measures. If it's been 48 hours since your last login, you'll be asked to provide both your fingerprint and your backup login method.

Your backup login method will also be required the next time you restart your phone.

CHAPTER SEVEN

HOW TO ENABLE FACE UNLOCK AND USE IT

Discover the ins and outs of using face unlock on your Pixel 8 or Pixel 8 Pro. Unlocking your Pixel 8 series will allow you to see your face. Pixel smartphones' security and privacy settings are where you can find the Face Unlock (Facial Recognition) options. One disadvantage is that someone who looks similar to you, like a brother, may unlock your Pixel phone. When configuring face unlock on the Google Pixel 8 or Pixel 8 Pro, be sure you wear the spectacles.

To access financial applications, make NFC transactions, utilize Google Wallet, and log in to apps, you may use the face unlock feature on your Google Pixel 8 series. Here we will go over the steps to enable face recognition for unlocking your Google Pixel devices.

The 8 Pro and 8 Pixel: How to Enable Face Unlock

The Pixel 8 and Pixel 8 Pro: How to Enable Face Unlock and Use It

In the app drawer of your Pixel device, tap the Settings app.

Press on "Security & privacy" after scrolling down.

Hit the "Unlock Device" button.

Unlock using Face ID or Fingerprint.

The use of a Password, PIN, or Pattern is required in the absence of a screen lock.

Turn on Face Unlock.

Start by clicking the "I Agree" button.

Get your Pixel ready for Face Unlock by holding it at eye level and positioning your face in the middle of the circle. Next, add the face by tilting your head up and down, or finish the job using tiles.

Hit the Finish button.

Your Google Pixel 8 can be unlocked just by looking at it. Additionally, you may confirm your identity in the app's settings and utilize face or fingerprint unlock to unlock your phone.

Google Pixel 8 and Pixel 8 Pro Fingerprint Settings

Enable fingerprint unlocking on your Pixel smartphone by configuring a fingerprint scanner. Enable many fingerprint sensors on your Pixel phone. When it comes to security, fingerprints are better than face unlock.

Go to the following menu: Settings > Security & privacy > Device unlock > Face & Fingerprint unlock > Fingerprint unlock Proceed as directed on the screen.

Will the Pixel 8 Support Face Recognition?

Yes, face unlock is compatible with the Pixel 8 and Pixel 8 Pro. Just by looking at your face, you can unlock your phone. Choose Face & Fingerprint unlock from the Device unlock menu in Settings > Security & privacy > Face unlock to enable face recognition. Proceed as directed on the screen.

Is It Possible to Lock Apps on the Google Pixel 8 Pro with Face Unlock?

The app's face unlock and fingerprint scanning features for Google Pixel handsets are no longer available for locking or unlocking.

INSTRUCTIONS FOR USING GOOGLE TRANSLATE ON THE PIXEL

Among Google's translation tools, the Live Translate app on newer Pixel phones is top-notch. Only the most current Pixel smartphones, such as the Pixel 6, Pixel 7, Pixel 8, and Pixel Fold, have access to Live Translate. It adds helpful translation tools that aid with real-time translation, going beyond what Google Translate can do.

Though it's only one more function among Google Translate's many, Live Translate packs a significant punch. Quickly and effortlessly translate between languages with the help of this handy tutorial.

How does Live Translate work?

The concept of Live Translate could be perplexing, even for long-time Google users. Even Google isn't sure; the Google Translate app's help page for Live Translate lists all of the functions that are accessible on all devices.

On the other hand, the one that can translate languages instantly is called Live Translate on Pixel smartphones. The fact that it is exclusive to Pixel smartphones is because it employs Google's Tensor processor. It does real-time audio and conversation translation. The newly released Pixel 8 Pro, running Android 14, makes using the phone, making calls, and watching movies more enjoyable. Visual representations of spoken or seen language are also available.

Live Translate has its flaws, just like any other translation program. Still, it's spot-on and more than enough to make it through a multilingual video.

The steps to enable Live Translate

Not all languages are supported by Live Translate. The list of languages that are compatible with live media is rather short: Japanese, German, English, Spanish, French, and Italian. Live Translate now supports twenty-one languages. After you turn on Live Translate, your Pixel will notify you of the functions that are compatible with that language.

1. Go to the app called Settings.
2. Find the System and tap on it.
3. Press on Live Translate.

An image of the Android settings menu.

4. In the Android system app, you can find the settings menu.
5. Enable the Live Translate feature.
6. Hit the "Add language" button.
7. Find the language you want to translate into and touch on it.

When a pop-up window appears, tap on Add language.

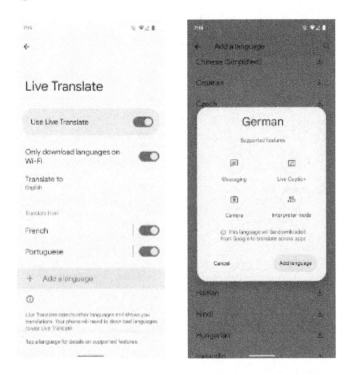

Android Live Translates configuration interface.

The linguistic capabilities of the Live Translate tool...

Using Live Translate should be no problem for you. After you've turned it on, we can go over some basic use instructions.

How to Live Translate

Live Translate is compatible with both spoken and written language. Google Translate may assist you in translating text from your camera or an in-person chat.

Prior to beginning the translation process, you must download the language. Just a few seconds should do it.

The ins and outs of messaging using Live Translate

If your Pixel smartphone recognizes that you're talking in a language other than English, a Google Translate logo will appear in the top right corner of the screen as a pop-up. By tapping here, Live Translate may be activated.

You may have to manually re-activate the pop-up if you turned off translation or if it doesn't show (sometimes this occurs when there isn't enough text on-screen). After copying the text, go to the pop-up window and choose the Translate copied text button.

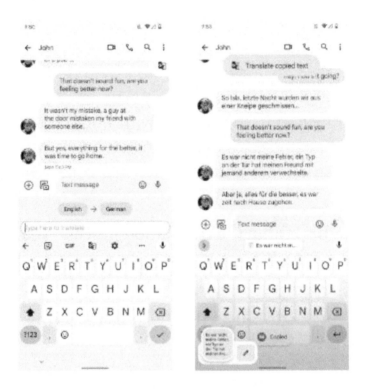

A white and blue text message exchange.

When you switch it on, a window will appear at the top of your screen. From there, you may choose the language that will be shown when you receive an SMS. Begin typing to begin translating your content. You are able to preview the translated content before submitting it since it shows above your draft in real-time.

A dialogue in text message format displaying the supported languages.

Here we see an example of a discussion being translated from English to German by text messaging.

- The process of translating text from English to German is shown in a conversational text message.
- To disable or customize Live Translate, press the arrow pointing downwards next to the languages.

All talks in that language, not just the present one will be affected by these settings.

- It will ask you to ask to translate if it notices a new language shown on the screen. Every new communication does not trigger a prompt.

Detects messages in that language and automatically translates them.

Stay away from translations: Saves Live Translate's language settings. To enable it again, go back to the Live Translate settings page. Additionally, you may reach this by pressing on More Settings located at the very bottom of this window.

How to configure Live Translate for messages.

Instructions for using Live Translate with audio

Closed captioning in English, French, German, Italian, Japanese, and Spanish is generated automatically by your Pixel device. The other party will be informed that you are using Live Captions if you want to do so during a call.

1. Press the phone's side-mounted volume button to enable live captions.
2. Press the Live Caption icon that appears under the on-screen volume controls.
3. Live Translate allows you to translate in real-time.

Thanks to Google's advancements in AI technology, Live Translate represents a significant leap forward in translation technology. Although this function is now only available on the Pixel 6, 7, 8, and Pixel Fold, we anticipate that it will be included in all of Google's next smartphones.

HOW TO CHANGE THE SETTINGS ON THE GOOGLE PIXEL PHONE CAMERA

There are a plethora of options for how you may record memories with the camera on your Google Pixel phone. But if you don't know which ones to turn on and which ones to turn off, juggling all of them may be a pain. If you own a Google Pixel phone, this tutorial will teach you everything you need to know to take the best photos possible by navigating the camera settings.

Launch your camera app and look for the settings option. From there, you can toggle the camera functions on and off. Typically, a gear or three dots will stand for it. The camera's settings menu may be accessed by tapping this icon. You can discover a list of the functions that are accessible in the camera settings. While some functions may be activated automatically, others may need to be set up.

Turning on Google Pixel Camera Features Launch the Camera app: Start up your Google Pixel phone's camera app. The camera icon in the app drawer or on the home screen may be used for this purpose.

To access the camera's settings, open the app and look for the gear icon. In most cases, you may find it on the top or side of the screen, and it generally looks like a gear or three dots. The camera's menu of options may be accessed by tapping this symbol.

Discover What's New: After you go into the settings, you'll see a rundown of all the functions that your camera has to offer. Features such as High Dynamic Range (HDR), Night Sight, Portrait Mode, Panorama, and others may be available.

Choose the function You Want: In the settings menu, choose the item that corresponds to the function you want to activate. Tap on it. To do this, you may need to choose an option or flip a switch.

You can confirm that a feature is activated on your camera by looking for an icon or indication on the UI.

Now that the option is enabled, you may test it out for yourself. Take a picture in different lighting conditions to see the effects of HDR, for example.

You may personalize the fast access menu in several camera applications if you want to. The camera screen usually displays this option as an icon. You have the option to prioritize the features you use the most by making them instantly accessible.

Keep Up-to-Date: Always check your phone's app store for updates. With software updates, you might get better camera functions and a whole lot more. If you want to stay up-to-date with all the possibilities, you should update your device often.

Learn by Doing: Spend some time getting to know each feature. By experimenting with the features, you may learn how they function and how they influence your images.

If you've made a lot of changes and would want to start again, you can usually find a "Reset to Default" or "Restore Settings" option in camera applications. All settings will be restored to their default values.

You may deactivate features by going back to the settings menu and selecting the ones you no longer want to use. Pressing on it will turn it off.

Turning Off Google Pixel Camera Features

Turning off the camera on a Google Pixel phone is as easy as pie. This is a detailed tutorial:

- Press the camera icon on your Google Pixel phone's home screen or app drawer to open the camera app.
- To access the camera's settings, open the app and look for the gear icon. You may find this icon—which looks like a gear or three dots—either at the top or around the borders of the camera interface. The camera's menu of options may be accessed by tapping this symbol.
- Find the list of camera functions by navigating to functions in the settings menu. Night Sight, Panorama, Portrait Mode, High Dynamic Range, and other capabilities may be among them.
- Turn Off the App You Want: In the settings menu, you'll see an option to turn off a particular app function. To disable the function, you may need to flick a switch.
- You can confirm that a feature has been removed by watching for the corresponding icon or

indication to vanish from your camera interface after you've disabled it.

- After you've disabled the function, try taking some images to see whether it has taken effect. After you disable a feature, it should no longer affect your photographs.

HOW TO SNAP BETTER PHOTOS WITH THE GOOGLE PIXEL

After establishing that the Pixel's camera is among the finest in its class, we now reveal the tricks to maximizing its performance.

A little familiarity with the camera app is in order before you can start snapping amazing images with your brand-new Google Pixel.

Once you make a few little adjustments, you'll be just as comfortable as with Google's Camera app. Anyone switching from an iPhone or another Android device will quickly get used to it.

To maximize your photography experience with the Google Pixel, consider the following eight suggestions:

Access the camera in a flash from any location

For Samsung devices, the shortcut to launch the camera is two presses of the home button. With iOS 10, Apple introduced a new way to open the camera: a fast swipe to the left on the home screen.

Google utilizes the lock/power button on the Pixel. This capability was introduced with the 2015 Nexus smartphones and is now available on the Pixel lineup, which is great.

Even if your phone is locked or you're in the middle of writing an email, you can access the camera app by double-pressing the power button.

Twist your wrist a second time

A button just to the left of the shutter release allows you to choose between the front and back cameras, and there's also a snazzy new Moves gesture that you can utilize while snapping a picture.

To toggle between the phone's cameras, mimic the gesture of twisting a door handle and twisting your wrist twice while using the camera app. You may return to the previous camera by twisting it again.

In the Moves area of the Settings app, you can find the new function turned on by default. If you want to disable it, you can also watch an animated lesson that explains how to utilize it.

Modes for shooting are rather obscure

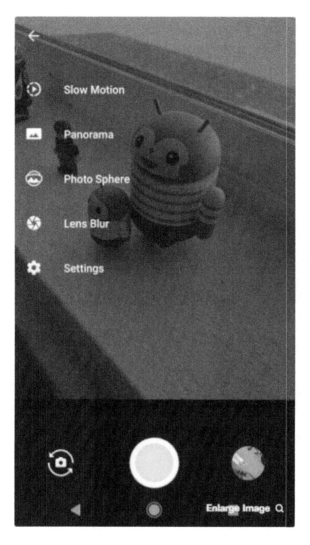

Picture of google-pixel-shooting-scenes.jpg

Switching between shooting modes on the Pixel could be a little difficult for iOS users used to seeing them all at once.

So what's the secret? Locate the Settings button and a menu of available modes by swiping in from the screen's left side.

Slow motion, panorama, photo sphere, and lens blur are the current available photography modes.

Make use of the microphone button

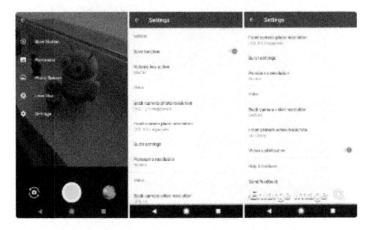

Google Pixel Camera Settings

By default, while you're using the camera app, the volume button will also release the shutter. But if you want to control zoom instead, or disable all camera-related functions from the button, you can do it under the camera settings.

Alter the image and video resolution

Go into the Pixel's Camera settings and choose a resolution that suits your needs for both still images and video.

Regardless of the rationale, Google is pre-installing the Pixel with 4K disabled. There is no need to disable 4K when you have free, limitless storage at full quality.

Stop the stabilization of the video.

The function is quite remarkable as long as you refrain from panning when capturing video with stabilization enabled. But stabilization makes the video hop around a lot whether you're walking about or moving the phone quite a bit. Some people find it tolerable. Some people find it bothersome.

There is an option on the camera where you may disable video stabilization.

Is it better to manually produce a GIF or not?

Pressing and holding the shutter button causes the camera to take many shots at once.

The camera software on the Pixel only mimics Google Photos in its tendency to merge many burst shots into one dynamic panorama.

You may turn off the function in the Camera's settings if you're not a fan of the animated effects.

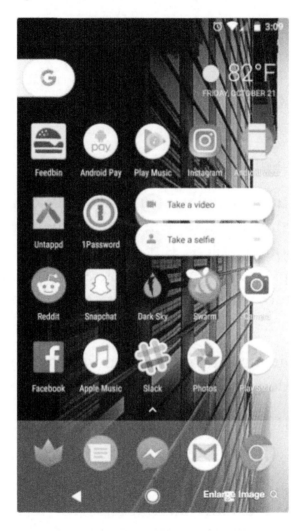

Picture of a shortcut for the Pixel camera app.

Remember that you may get shortcuts to shooting a selfie or recording a video without using the app by long-pressing on the camera icon.

CHAPTER EIGHT

HOW TO USE THE GOOGLE PHOTOS MAGIC ERASER AND CAMOUFLAGE TOOLS

Of all the gallery applications available, Google Photos is one of the most popular. It has great editing features and makes it easy to organize and share your memories. One tool that may easily remove unwanted elements and distractions from a picture is Magic Eraser. If you want to hide or erase unwanted elements from your images, it does the job. You may blend certain immovable elements from a picture with Magic Eraser's Camouflage masking tool.

You can access both of these features right from the Google Photos app, and they're both really straightforward to use. In case you're unfamiliar with them and are curious about how to use them to edit your images, this tutorial will walk you through the process step by step:

The Google Photos app is the only place you'll find the Magic Eraser and Camouflage tools. Users of the Pixel 6 and Pixel 7 series have free access to them, whereas users of other smartphones, such as the iPhone, are only able to use them if they have a Google One cloud storage plan.

An introduction to Google's Camouflage and Magic Eraser

1. To make changes to a photograph in Google Photos, find it in your library and then touch the Edit icon.
2. Pick Magic Eraser from the Tools menu.
3. Here you can see a toggle that lets you choose between two modes: Erase and Camouflage.
4. If you encounter any recommendations, choose Erase all or Camouflage all. Alternatively, you may manually erase or camouflage by drawing a circle or brush with your fingertips.

That's how simple the Camouflage and Magic Eraser are to use. You should be able to immediately see choices to erase or mask in Google Photos since it is really intelligent. Alternatively, you may quickly delete or conceal topics by manually selecting them.

How Google Photos' Magic Eraser and Camouflage Function Differ

Though they serve distinct functions, the two products are housed in the same Google Photos environment. Using Magic Eraser, you may completely delete any undesired subjects or objects from your images. Here's a case where we utilized Magic Eraser to remove some undesirable individuals from the subject's background:

The Magic Eraser tool intelligently pointed out these areas and recommended that we delete them to make the picture better.

However, the Camouflage tool is limited to desaturating or adding subdued colors in order to make disturbing items blend in better with the backdrop. The effects are modest and may change depending on the subject of the shot, but they are effective when the Magic Eraser fails to dissolve an item completely. To hide those stubborn items, try using Magic Eraser in a camouflage pattern. Desaturating or adding subdued hues will make them less obtrusive, allowing you to concentrate on the primary topic. Presently, examine this:

The OnePlus Buds Pro 2 earphones and their packaging are far less obtrusive in the right picture than in the left one. To make them less noticeable, we desaturated the red hue using the Camouflage option. Since the Magic Eraser left behind some residue when used to remove them fully, we found that the Camouflage tool worked better in this case.

Use Google Photos' editing features to make your images seem better.

In 2021, the Magic Eraser function was a major hit, and now in 2023, it's just as great and handy as ever. What makes it even better is that it is no longer limited to certain Pixel phones; with a Google One subscription, you can use it on almost every excellent smartphone available. Neither of these instruments is perfect, but they simplify applying adjustments that would normally need more expensive equipment and knowledge.

You may find a feature that allows you to eliminate undesirable items from photographs in Samsung's Gallery app. It's named Object Eraser. It fixes your photos quite well, and if you want to know which one is superior, you may compare Google Magic Eraser vs Samsung Object Eraser.

TIPS TO MAKE YOUR PHOTOS POP

Even though the cameras on our brand-new Pixel 7 and Pixel 7 Pro are top-notch, taking pictures is just the start of what these phones can do. Before sharing or looking back on our images, we all want them to seem perfect. Google Photos has a ton of great editing tools that are also very easy to use, all because of recent developments in machine intelligence.

Whether you're using Google images on a brand new Pixel 7 or an older phone, here are seven ways to make your images seem their best.

1. Use Photo Unblur to fix hazy photos

A new function exclusive to the Pixel 7 and Pixel 7 Pro, Photo Unblur makes it easy to restore focus to out-of-focus images with a few touches. By erasing noise and blur, Photo Unblur allows you to see the scene as vividly as you remember it. Plus, it's compatible with scanned photographs and photos shot with other phones or cameras, which is the cherry on top.

An animated comparison of the original image and the one after using Photo Unblur.

2. Use the Magic Eraser to eliminate any potential interruptions.

Last year, Magic Eraser was released with the ability to identify and remove photobombers, power lines, and poles that could be in the backdrop of your images. It just takes a few touches to get rid of them.

You have the option to either brush or circle the area you want to erase. You don't have to be exact since Magic Eraser will detect what you're attempting to erase.

Animated before and after images of a photograph with unwanted elements erased from the background using Magic Eraser Bonus Use the Magic Eraser to make an unwanted object blend in a little more rather than completely disappear. To make unwanted elements in your shot blend in with their surroundings, use Magic Eraser's Camouflage feature. With a few touches, the object's tones and hues will disappear into the background.

3. Use portrait blur to make your subject pop.

Use the Pixel Camera's portrait mode to bring forth your subject's best features. What if, however, you want to modify an older photo or just forgot to utilize it while taking the first shot? After taking a picture of a person, animal, dish, flower, or other subject, Google Photos' Portrait blur feature may automatically blur the backdrop.

The image of a butterfly perched on a flower was animated both before and after the addition of portrait blur.

4. Portrait light is a great tool for enhancing the lighting of faces.

If you're using an older phone or camera if the lighting isn't ideal, it might be challenging to get a nice image. You can quickly and simply enhance the lighting on faces using Portrait light, and you can even change the location and strength of the light to create your own unique style.

Portrait light is applied to a selfie before and after animation.

5. Use the HDR effect to make your photographs seem more balanced.

The finer details may be difficult to see in older photographs when the foreground is dark and the backdrop is light, or the other way around. To even things out, the HDR effect boosts contrast and brightness across the picture, allowing you to appreciate every detail.

6. Use sky ideas to change the mood and tone of your sunset photos.

There are probably a lot of sunset images in your collection that don't do justice to the splendor you experienced that day. Is there a way to give it new life so that it stands out? Take advantage of sky recommendations to give your golden hour photos a unique spin. To make your photo more shareable, you may alter its tone and mood by choosing from a variety of palettes that alter the sky's hue and contrast.

A time-lapse video showing the original and edited versions of a sunset photo.

7. Create shared artwork using the collage editor.

Use the new collage editor to create unique, shareable collages. Pixel users may choose from over 50 different styles and up to six photographs to utilize. Rearranging the arrangement is a breeze using the intuitive drag-and-drop controls, and you can tweak the appearance of each picture in the collage separately to get your desired effect.

This animation showcases the many styles available in Google Photos' collage editor.

Put your imagination to work and combine all of these elements to create a breathtaking picture that you can't wait to show off. After you've eliminated a backdrop photobomber, you may breathe new life into your memories by using Photo Unblur, Portrait light, and Portrait blur. An animated comparison of the original image and its subsequent processing using the tools Photo Unblur, Magic Eraser, Portrait Light, and Portrait Blur.

If you own a Pixel 7 or Pixel 7 Pro, Google Photos has everything you need to enhance your images or give them a unique twist. Start modifying your photos and then post them online using the hashtag #FixedOnPixel.

HOW TO TAKE SELFIES WITH YOUR GOOGLE PIXEL

There are two levels of magnification available when taking a selfie; by default, the phone uses a 1x zoom. Use the 0.7x toggle to get the camera's default field of view. Each setting produces 10 megapixels of output.

Compared to the Pixel 8's fixed-focus arrangement, the Pixel 8 Pro's autofocusing selfie camera doesn't provide any significant benefit for images taken at arm's length. However, the Pro does offer a little improvement in natural background blur. With that exception, the selfies are almost interchangeable.

Assuming your 0.7x selfies aren't taken in a brightly lit room, you should be able to get decent clarity and definition. However, if your face is backlit, the quantity of pores you can count will be limited due to the gain required to increase the exposure to a more agreeable level and the noise reduction that follows. We don't have many complaints about the color reproduction or skin tones, save from the occasional little white balance error.

Here are some example selfies shot with the Google Pixel 8 Pro: 0.7x, f/2.2, ISO 45, 1/280s. Here are some example selfies shot with the Google Pixel 8 Pro: 0.7x, f/2.2, ISO 75, 1/20s. Images captured with the Google Pixel 8 Pro: 0.7x magnification, f/2.2 aperture, ISO 111 shutter speed, 1/30s exposure.

If you want a tighter frame, you can get away with shooting at the 1x zoom option, albeit it does somewhat reduce absolute sharpness.

Here are some selfie examples from the Google Pixel 8 Pro: 1x - f/2.2, ISO 51, 1/168s.

selfies

In addition to the "mainstream" 30 frames per second, the four cameras on the Pixel 8 Pro can shoot video at a maximum of 4K60. The front-facing camera is also available in 24fps mode. H.265 is an option in the options menu, while h.264 is the default. Another choice is 10-bit HDR recording, which may go as high as 4K30. In every setting, you'll also get stability.

Video recordings made with the Pixel 8 Pro's primary camera look stunning. The film is quite detailed and doesn't change much between 24 and 30 frames per second, with the exception of 60 frames per second, where the clarity is somewhat reduced. We also don't have any complaints about global factors such as dynamic range, white balance, and color saturation.

While still passable, footage captured at 2x zoom is much worse quality overall, and close-up analysis makes the upscaling obvious. Although 1080p may be the better choice, they aren't so terrible that they're useless if you want 4K for consistency.

Once again, the 5x telephoto captures high-quality video without sacrificing detail in either the 24 or 30fps modes; the only difference is that the 60fps mode seems identical down to the individual pixels. Everything is fine, really: the exposure is spot on, the colors are fantastic, and the dynamic range is broad and pleasant.

videos

When it comes to the video quality, the ultra-wide gave us mixed impressions. Impressively, it manages to capture outstanding detail across all three frame rates, surpassing even the Pixel 8's. Not only that, the highlights and shadows are well rendered, and the dynamic range is enough.

The white balance on this camera isn't great; the balcony picture came out looking too warm and reddish. The stabilization samples (detailed below) also showed some evidence of it, thus it wasn't exclusive to the balcony scene. Plus, we didn't see it in the still images, so it seems to be a problem exclusive to the video. It's not a huge problem, but it will be noticeable, especially when comparing side by side.

Even in low light, the primary camera on the Pixel 8 Pro manages to capture films with respectable quality. Additionally commendable are the excellent dynamic range, well-balanced whites, and pleasing color saturation. Although it's still not as noticeable as what we often see on iPhones, the ghosting from point-light sources is the one thing that's a little unpleasant.

The telephoto lens has certain problems when used at night, the most significant of which being its focus-hunting propensity; nevertheless, it will likely perform much better with shallower depth-of-field situations. Additionally, there is astigmatism, which is seen as these brilliant streaks emanating from point lights; but, to be fair, this is a characteristic shared by the majority of telescopic lenses used in low light. The Pixel 8 Pro's zoom camera takes good pictures when it focuses, and you should be happy with the results if you don't look at individual pixels. Under these circumstances, the camera's dynamic range is quite impressive, and the colors are also difficult to criticize.

Once again, the Pixel 8 Pro's ultrawide camera excels in low-light video capture compared to the non-Pro models. Impressively detailed, it rivals the ultrawide lens on the iPhone 15 Pro (Max). However, the Pixel's dynamic range isn't up to scratch, and the result is rather harsh shadows and highlights.

Once again, the Pixel 8 Pro's ultrawide camera excels in low-light video capture compared to the non-Pro models. Impressively detailed, it rivals the ultrawide lens on the iPhone 15 Pro (Max). However, the Pixel's dynamic range isn't up to scratch, and the result is rather harsh shadows and highlights.

TRICKS ON USING THE GOOGLE CAMERA

Take pictures of the ocean or sky and replace them

You may now create a new sky for your pictures using the new Magic Edit function. Alternatively, you might fake golden hour.

Launch the Google Photos app and choose the image you want to modify. Next, touch the purple star-shaped Magic Edit button that appears in the corner.

Select "Sky," "Golden Hour," or "Water" from the drop-down menu that appears on the subsequent screen by tapping the colored pencil icon.

Magic Edit for Pixel 8

A new backdrop will be automatically generated when you've made your selection. It can be a breathtaking sunset, more mesmerizing water, or just a sky that's always changing. You have the option to produce new results if you are unhappy with the ones you get. After you've found happiness, just

Reposition and magnify your subjects in the camera.

Selecting the subject of your shot and then repositioning and enlarging it to make it stand out is another neat magic edit function.

Just open a picture in your editor and hit that magic edit button again to start using it. Now you may touch the topic to make them the focus.

You can pinch to zoom in or out, move the topic around, and hold it to make it bigger or smaller. After you're satisfied, click the arrow in the bottom corner to see the alternatives it generated for you. Mark as a favorite.

Artificial intelligence wallpaper creation for the Pixel 8

Asking Google to design a wallpaper for you based on your preferences is a neat function. To begin, press and hold the home screen wallpaper until you get the "Wallpaper and Style" menu. After selecting "More wallpapers" on the subsequent screen, you will be able to locate the AI wallpaper choice at the page's top. Press it.

Select a theme to begin, and then look for an underlined command on the screen that follows. Before hitting "create wallpaper," tap on any of the highlighted words to get other choices. It will now create wallpapers to suit your needs. Mark as a favorite.

Use face unlock to unlock applications

Updated hardware from Google now includes the ability to employ face unlock for app and payment authentication. Activating it is as simple as going to Settings > Security and privacy. After you choose "Device Unlock," press "Face and Fingerprint Unlock" on the subsequent screen. Proceed by entering your PIN.

If you haven't done so before, add a Face Unlock scan and follow the on-screen instructions. Turning on "Verify that it's you in apps" will allow your phone to unlock and verify inside apps using your face scan.

Magic Audio Remover

Google has implemented an AI-powered function that may edit out unwanted noises from your movies. Simply capture your video as usual to utilize it. After opening the video, go to the "Edit" menu and choose "Audio." From there, push the "Audio Eraser" option. While it detects the noises, touch on the unwanted background noise and drag the slider to lower the level of the desired sound.

Pixel 8, now playing on a 6. Recognizing songs automatically

If your Google Pixel phone is able to pick up ambient music, it will show the name and artist of the song on the lock screen. Find it in the Settings menu, then under Display, and finally turn it on.

Upon reaching the "Now Playing" page, you will see an option to "Identify songs." Toggle this checkbox. You also have the option to look for music that it didn't recognize right away if you so choose. By selecting "now playing history," you may also see your whole history if you so choose.

The pixel 8—notifications that flash

Notifications that flash

When alerts are received, you have the option to have the camera's LED light up. Activating the 'Camera flash' feature is as easy as going to the 'Flash notifications' section of the Accessibility menu in Settings.

A Reward for the Holiday

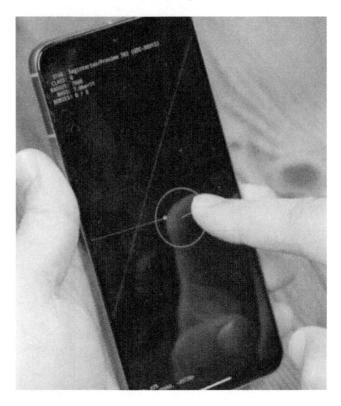

An Easter egg, concealed in the Settings, is included in every new version of Android. Navigate to "About Phone" in the Settings menu, press it, and then continue scrolling until you see "Android Version" on the subsequent screen. After you choose it, on the next screen, touch "Android Version" a number of times till a visual appears.

Locate the graphic in the screen's center and press and hold. It will display stars racing past while vibrating. If you maintain your grip, a minigame will load.

Your little spacecraft may now be controlled by tapping and dragging in any direction. You may guide your spacecraft to the closest star, with the center at location '0,0', by referring to the coordinates and thrust in the page's footer. You will slam into a large, brilliant star when you reach that point.

CHAPTER NINE

HOW TO USE THE DUAL DISPLAY MODE

Mastering the art of screen sharing will enable you to run many applications in the background simultaneously.

This guide will teach you the ropes, so you can:

- Use Picture-in-picture • Adjust window size • Access split screen
- Take notes while viewing a movie, surf the web, and check your email all at once with the use of split screen capabilities.
- Launch the Split Screen feature
1. Swipe up from the bottom of the screen while holding your finger on the screen to browse recent applications.
2. Pick the app you want to use, and then go to the Split screen.

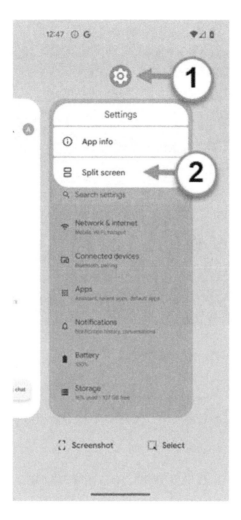

The ability to split the screen will only be available in supported applications.

3. In the bottom box, choose the app you want to show.

The example only made use of the Calendar and Contacts applications.

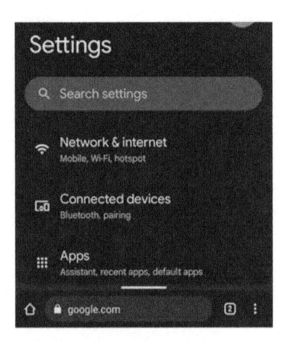

Size the window as needed.

To adjust the height of the screen's divide, click and hold the symbol in the center of the screen, and then let go.

You may launch an app in its entirety by dragging the divider symbol to the bottom or top of the screen. Just make sure you choose the correct app.

Split screen mode is disabled.

Starting at the bottom of the screen, swipe up while keeping your finger pressed on it. To remove it, just swipe up on the split-screen window.

Incorporate picture-in-picture

When you're in fullscreen mode in Google applications like Maps, Meet, YouTube, or Chrome, swipe up from the bottom of the screen. The program will appear in the screen's corner as a picture-in-picture window.

Important: Feel free to choose and move the window around as you want. Some applications have picture-in-picture enabled by default. To find out which applications are compatible with Picture-in-picture, you may do the following: use two fingers to slide down from the notification bar, then tap the settings icon. From there, choose applications, then special app access. Finally, tap Picture-in-picture. A list of all the apps that support Picture-in-picture will be shown.

Make Utilize Multiple Windows

The terms "multi-window" and "split top" or "split screen" are similar.

You may run many programs in parallel on the same screen by using the "Multi window" capability.

'Multi window' isn't supported by every computer program.

In order to see all currently open applications on a Home screen, you may slide up and hold from the bottom of the screen.

1. Find your desired app by scrolling left or right.
2. At the top of the panel, you should see the icon of an app like Chrome, Settings, Camera, etc. After tapping on it, choose Split screen.
3. The options could change according to the app you choose.

New Applications

Select the second app to see from the Recent applications screen.

You can access all of your open applications by swiping up and holding them from the bottom of the screen; from there, you can touch on the one you want to switch to. To dismiss the split-screen mode, drag the horizontal bar to the top or bottom of the screen.

Slide the horizontal bar between the applications to increase or decrease their size.

Multi-Monitor Display

ACTIVATE YOUR GOOGLE PIXEL PHONE'S SECURITY AND EMERGENCY FUNCTIONS

There are life-saving emergency functions built into Pixel phones. Their use is explained here.

You should consider yourself fortunate to own a Google Pixel, since emergencies may occur anywhere and at any moment. It has built-in safety mechanisms that might end up saving your life or someone you care about's life in an emergency.

The most recent Pixel phones have a capability called Emergency SOS call, in addition to the usual Emergency Dial button and a few other features. But their precise use is unclear. Ok, let's check it out.

What Is the Meaning of an Emergency Quick Call?

Android phones have long had emergency information accessible via the lock screen, eliminating the need to unlock the handset. From it, you may view previously entered medical information, make emergency calls (even when the phone is locked), and even use it to dial 911 without cell coverage provided you have specific applications.

Pressing and holding the power button, followed by hitting the Emergency Call button, will bring up this menu on any Google Pixel phone. If you push the power button five times on the Pixel 4, 5, or 6, an emergency call will be instantly made.

Methods for Making Critical Calls on the Google Pixel

New Google Pixel

You never know when you may need your Google Pixel's medical data or SOS emergency calls function, so be sure to enable and set both. When that moment arrives, it could be too late to create this setup.

To prepare your Pixel for medical emergencies, follow these instructions. Without access to other information on the phone, emergency services will be able to see data such as blood type, allergies, weight, organ donation status, and contact information. Additionally, you may make an Emergency SOS call on the more recent Pixels (4, 5, and 6). This is the way:

1. To access the safety and emergency settings, use the Settings app.
2. Select the SOS emergency button.
3. After that, choose "Turn on Emergency SOS." 3. When you utilize this function, your phone will automatically contact 911 and play a loud alert. I can disable it for you if you'd like.
4. Before a genuine emergency occurs, choose which emergency services you want activated. In an emergency, you have the option to phone 911, record a brief video, or notify a pre-selected emergency contact of your whereabouts and other details.
5. You have the option to modify the default number for calling emergency services, however it is currently set to 911.
• Pick and pick the details to send with emergency contacts by clicking the corresponding button.

- You may easily share recorded footage with those you've designated as emergency contacts by selecting the "Record emergency video" option.

Making an Emergency SOS Call Contact the

Pressing the power button rapidly five times will launch the emergency SOS call. Assuming you haven't disabled it, your alarm will sound. In the event of an emergency, your designated contact may get a video message, your information will be shared with them, and 911 may be dialed, depending on the settings you made in the previous section.

After you've pressed the power button five times, you may cancel the Emergency SOS call by swiping across the bottom of the screen.

Can You Tell Me the Drawbacks of the SOS Call Emergency Function?

One potential drawback is that your Pixel might inadvertently contact all of your emergency contacts and dial 911 if its power button is very sensitive. Reportedly, this has happened with certain models to some consumers.

You should get a case cover that has the power button already attached. The majority of users have reported that this has resolved the problem of accidentally dialing 911. Alternatively, you may disable the Emergency SOS call service and continue using the standard Pixel capabilities in an emergency.

Essential Safety Functions for Every Pixel Model

All Pixel devices have the standard Android emergency settings, while the newer ones only have the Emergency SOS option. This is how they are turned on:

1. To get the emergency information, use the Settings app and go to About phone.
2. Adjust to your liking. Detection and alarms, Emergency reactions, and Contacts and details may all be edited here.
- By going to the Settings menu and choosing "Emergency response," you'll be able to enable the ability to communicate some information with your emergency contacts.
- To make changes to your emergency contact information and medical records, go to Contacts and info.
- Detection and notifications allow you to enable features like public emergency warnings, detection of natural catastrophes, and auto accident detection.

If you are involved in a traffic collision, car crash detection will be useful. If you do, and your phone senses that you've been in an accident and aren't moving, it will automatically contact emergency services.

Just like the Apple Watch's fall function, this one works by sending you a notification to make sure you're OK after an accident.

After a respectable amount of time has passed with no answer, the phone will contact emergency services using your location and get in touch with a relative you've chosen.

The Individual Security Program

Alternatively, you may use the Pixel Personal Safety App to make all of the aforementioned adjustments. The app's safety sharing feature allows you to notify your emergency contacts of your current position in the event that you feel threatened but do not yet have a medical emergency.

Additionally, there is a safety check feature that may be used as a timer. You may set the timer to notify your emergency contacts if you don't respond after a certain amount of time.

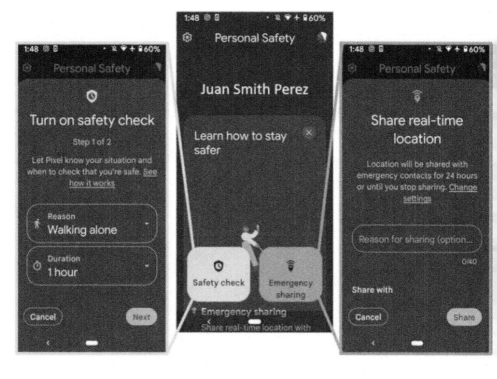

Services such as safety checks and emergency sharing may be exemplified by the Pixel-3 Personal Safety App.

Procedures for Making Emergency Calls

If you have an older Pixel, you won't be able to use the five-press power button feature to trigger an emergency SOS call, but you may still make such a call without entering a PIN, pattern, fingerprint, or password. This is how it operates:

If you want to access your data and emergency contacts on your Google Pixel, tap and hold the power button for a few seconds until you see the restart or shutdown screen.

1. Emergency, Shutdown, and Restart will be the three choices that show up. To access the various choices for making emergency calls and contacting SOS, press the Emergency button.
2. Your Google Pixel will display a keyboard along with an emergency information button at the top of the screen. Pressing this button will bring up the emergency details you've specified. Everything from your name and address to your blood type, allergies, medications, and emergency contacts should be included.

Trust Your Pixel With Peace Of Mind

Now that you are familiar with the Pixel phone's safety features, you can rest certain that your phone can assist you in a genuine emergency. Sharing this information might help you and your loved one feel more secure and in charge if you are concerned about them.

Trust Your Pixel With Peace Of Mind

Now that you are familiar with the Pixel phone's safety features, you can rest certain that your phone can assist you in a genuine emergency. Sharing this information might help you and your loved one feel more secure and in charge if you are concerned about them.

1. Some smartphone makers, like Samsung and LG, have offered one-handed modes for a while now. These modes allow you to use your thumb to access on-screen material that would be difficult or impossible to reach with two hands. With Android 12, Google has finally released its version for Pixel phones, catching up to the competition.

2. Apple wasn't the first to provide a one-handed option; the feature was dubbed Reachability and it was included in the iPhone 6 and later versions of smartphones. This mode moved the whole screen down the display so that the top half could be more readily reached. Even earlier, in Android 4.3, there was an accessibility option that shrank the whole screen for the Samsung Galaxy Note 3 phablet.

3. Don't Miss: The Most Current and Comprehensive List of Android 12 Supporting and Upcoming Devices

HOW TO USE THE ONE-HAND MODE ON YOUR PIXEL PHONE

Users with smaller hands who still want access to the powerful hardware and excellent specifications found in smartphones with bigger screens will love these accessibility features. Even someone like myself who has bigger hands and doesn't want to strain themselves may appreciate this: it's much simpler to tap a button near the center of the screen than one at the very top.

Google Pixel 3 and later devices running Android 12 have one-handed mode built in, although it's not turned on by default. Other original equipment manufacturer (OEM) handsets that did not previously have their own version may have it enabled automatically after upgrading to Android 12, albeit this varies from model to model. If your gadget is one of them, you may see how to utilize it in Step # below.

Select the "One-Handed Mode"

For smartphones running vanilla Android 12, including the Google Pixel, unlocking one-handed mode is a breeze. If your phone isn't running the official Android 12 software, be aware that skinned software can change how the function works or remove it completely.

Select "One-handed mode" from the list of gestures in the System menu under Settings.

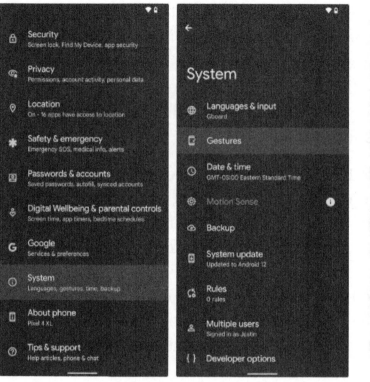

If the option to "Use one-handed mode" is not already selected, you may activate it by toggling the switch on that screen.

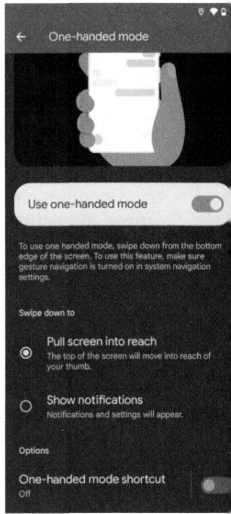

For the one-handed shortcut to function, your device must have "Gesture navigation" activated. Verify that it is enabled by navigating to Settings > System > Gestures > System navigation.

Select All Notifications or Screens

Several choices for personalizing the functionality may be found within the one-handed mode parameters. You may make the top half of the screen more accessible by swiping down from the bottom edge of the screen; the default option, "Pull screen into reach," will do just that.

On the other hand, you have the option to choose "Show notifications," which would bring the quick settings and notifications panel down from the top of the screen. You may still utilize the old approach of swiping down from the top of the screen with one finger anytime you like; this method is just as effective. In one-handed mode, however, you won't have to shift the phone around in your palm so your thumb can reach the top.

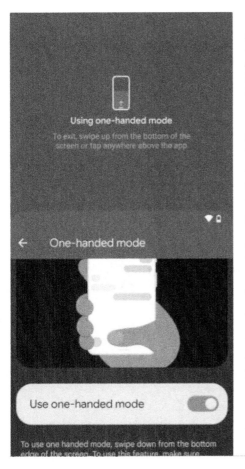

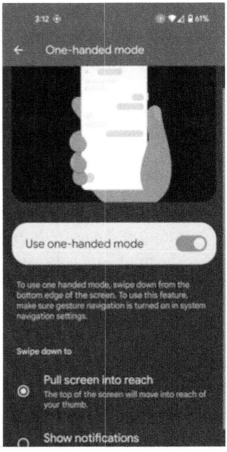

In earlier versions of Android 12, the one-handed mode setting allowed you to choose between two options: "Exit when switching apps," which would restore the screen to normal anytime you switched apps, and "Timeout," which would allow you to choose the length for how long the screen would return to normal.

The first is superfluous since you already have to shut the view that you can access before you can switch programs. Both of these were eliminated, and the "Time to take action" option under Accessibility's "Timing controls" is irrelevant when using one-handed mode.

If desired, choose an accessibility option.

Because the swipe gesture isn't always reliable, you may make one-handed mode your accessibility shortcut—just as with many of Android 12's other innovations.

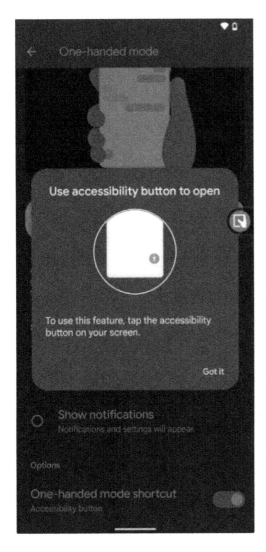

The accessibility shortcut may be accessed by toggling the "One-handed mode shortcut" filter. A pop-up will appear, either instructing you to utilize the on-screen accessibility button or the long-press gesture on the volume buttons, depending on how you selected the accessibility option.

You may quickly switch between triggers by pressing the "One-handed mode shortcut." With the "Tap accessibility button" or "Hold volume keys" options shown in the pop-up, choose your preferred method and then "Save." If you like, you may even enable both options. Accessibility button settings allow you to modify the size, fading, and transparency of the tool by selecting "More options" under the accessibility button option.

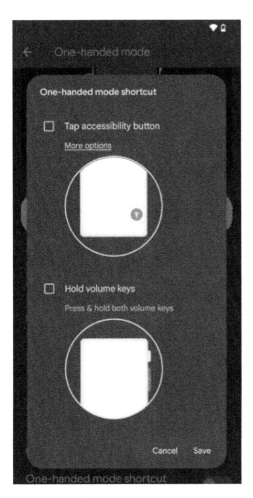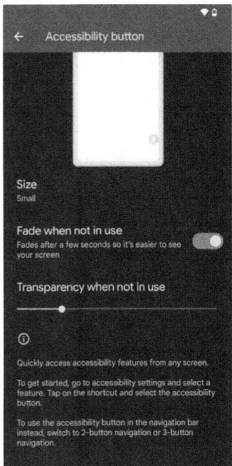

Switch to One-Handed Mode

Once you've enabled and customized one-handed mode, you'll be able to utilize it with almost all portrait-oriented apps. You can't use the one-handed mode in landscape mode.

Making Use of the Swipe Motions

Swiping down on the center of the bottom border of the screen will make the top of your screen more accessible. If all goes according to plan, your screen's contents will resize to fit your thumb's reach. Entering the mode could be a bit of a pain, particularly if you're trying to swipe over any moving material.

When using one-handed mode, swiping down on the center of the bottom edge of the screen will reveal fast settings and notifications instead of dragging the current app's screen down.

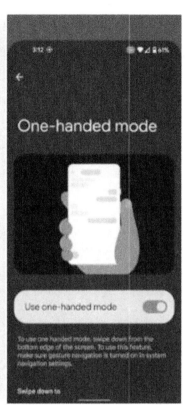

Cutting Out the Middleman

A one-handed mode shortcut is available by either the accessibility shortcut button on the screen or by long-pressing the volume up and down keys simultaneously. Depending on your preferences, this will either minimize the app or bring up the notification and quick settings.

If the shortcut takes you to the bottom of an app's screen, you may use it again to bring it to the top.

After you've configured the shortcut for notifications, you can access the fast settings by tapping the accessibility shortcut button or by long-pressing the volume buttons twice. Notifications and quick settings will still be visible after pressing either shortcut three times.

Additionally, you'll need to "Turn on" the one-handed mode shortcut in order to proceed if you've never used the volume buttons accessibility shortcut before.

WHAT DRAINS THE BATTERY LIFE OF THE GOOGLE PIXEL

Are you experiencing rapid battery loss on your Google Phone? If your Google Pixel's battery dies suddenly, there are a few things you should know. If you want to know what to do since the issue might be software- or hardware-related, keep reading!

Initial Stages

To rule out a software glitch, restarting your phone is an excellent first step.

- Maintain a 30-second press and hold on the Power button. Pressing Restart after holding the Power button is necessary for some Pixels.

Recent Android versions have fixed a number of issues with power and battery life, so updating your phone is essential.

- To check for updates, open the Settings app and go to System > System Update.

Applications that allow users to multitask

The battery dies quicker when you use many applications at once since they all need a lot of electricity. Put unneeded applications, such as video or gaming ones, to sleep. Excessive use of power-intensive applications, such as GPS navigation, gaming, and video recording, may quickly deplete the battery.

- Simply swipe up from the bottom of the screen and choose Clear all to terminate all currently active applications. To get the most out of your phone, it's a good idea to exit all applications every so often.

Furthermore, to slow down the power drain, turn off WiFi and Bluetooth.

- Swipe down from the top of your phone's screen and toggle the Bluetooth icon to deactivate Bluetooth.

Relying Too Much on Apps

Apps that use a lot of battery life in general should have their background use limited.

- Tap on Battery in your phone's Settings menu. From there, choose Battery use. Here you can see all the applications and how much power they used in the last 24 hours. Simply tap on each program to see how much power it is using and to enable or disable Battery Optimization.

Video Recording and Camera App

The battery life of the phone will be negatively impacted while recording HD video for an extended duration. You can prolong the life of your phone and keep it from dying on you by charging it as you use it.

There are a lot of capabilities in the Google Camera app, and most of them make the battery drain and background service run faster.

- Disable Google Lens recommendations, Social sharing, Frequent Faces, Framing Suggestions, and Exposure in the Google Camera settings. Go to the advanced menu and turn off these options: Management of RAW and JPEG files, as well as capabilities for social media exploration.

Very Hot Conditions

Is your phone prone to overheating? If you use your phone often and then expose it to direct sunlight, its battery life will be drastically reduced.

- Turn down the screen's brightness, put the gadget in a cool, shady spot, and wait for it to cool down. Additionally, it is recommended to power down the Pixel until it has cooled down.

Deterioration of Batteries

The phone may overheat and not get enough power from a worn-out battery.

- Try replacing the battery and following the instructions that come with it.

The cause of your Google Pixel's overheating problem and possible solutions

CHAPTER TEN

PIXEL GOOGLE'S OVERHEATING PROBLEM

How come my Google PixelTM is overheating? Perhaps you've pondered this same thing when you've ever reached for your phone and felt as warm and ready as a pizza.

In most cases, the culprit is that your gadget has been overworked. There are a lot of things that might cause your phone to overheat, such as conversing on the phone for long periods of time or having a lot of applications running in the background. The battery and other components of your Pixel smartphone might eventually be damaged by it.

Rest assured, however. If you want to maintain your phone in good working order, we have some simple advice for you. From security to repairs, Asurion can take care of all your computer care requirements. If your Google Pixel is becoming too hot, try these solutions.

Put your Pixel down and let it charge for a time.

As it charges, it's natural for your phone to become a little hotter than usual. However, using more energy—and making it hotter—is required while speaking with a buddy or surfing the web. If you can refrain from using your cellphone while it's charging, you should see a significant improvement.

Turn down the brightness on your screen

Increasing the brightness of your screen can put extra strain on your battery and cause it to overheat. The inverse is also correct. Turn down the brightness of your screen to save power.

In this way:

1. Go to the Settings menu.
2. Go to the Display menu and then Touch the Brightness level. Make the necessary adjustments to the slider.
3. To enable adaptive brightness, which will automatically change the screen's brightness, tap on the corresponding button and then toggle it on.
4. Next, choose the Dark theme. By making the backdrop darker, this option will improve your phone's battery life and keep it from overheating.

Spend less time acting as a wireless hotspot.

Sharing your PixelTM hotspot with pals is great, but it may potentially lead to overheating, particularly if you're simultaneously doing things like browsing the web. Use the hotspot function sparingly if you're experiencing problems with overheating. Do not assign additional tasks to your Pixel while you are using it as a hotspot.

Evaluate your applications

Is there an app that causes your Pixel to overheat? Your phone may not be able to manage the amount of stress the app causes. On the other hand, it may be draining the battery quickly. Your phone will suffer in any case. Give the problematic app an update. Remove it and try downloading the program again to see if it helps if there isn't an update available.

Remove all data from your cache.

A portion of your phone's storage called the cache partition is reserved for temporary files that facilitate quicker and simpler device use. Even if you don't access or use such files often, they nonetheless accumulate over time. If your phone isn't using any unnecessary data, clearing its cache will remove it.

Unlike other AndroidTM phones, the Google Pixel does not have a cache sector that can be manually cleared. To have the same result, however, you may erase the cache partitions of the individual applications.

Here are the steps to remove an app's cache:

1. Launch Settings.
2. To choose an app, tap on Apps.
3. Press the Storage & cache button.
4. Use the Clear storage or Clear cache buttons.

The Files app also has a Clean option that you may use to remove temporary program data.

Keep your operating system up-to-date.

Has it not worked? Your software might be the source of the issue. Make sure your Pixel is up-to-date by checking for updates.

1. Go to the Settings menu.
2. Click on System and then choose System update.
3. Press the Update button. If your OS is current, you should receive a notification that says "Current software is up to date." If an update is available, you may download it by following the instructions.
4. Press OK when you are prepared to install.

Start using your Pixel again when the update is complete to see if it overheats.

See whether the Pixel works in Safe Mode.

Utilizing Safe Mode compels your device to execute just mandatory or pre-installed applications. To find out why your phone is becoming too hot, you should wait for anything that can trigger this problem.

To boot your Pixel into safe mode, follow these steps:

1. For a few seconds, press and hold the Power and Volume Up keys on your Pixel 6 or later phone. Next, choose Power off.

- For a few seconds, press and hold the Power button on your Pixel 5a or older phone. Next, choose Power off.
2. To power up your phone again after it has turned off, press and hold the power button. The words "Safe mode" ought to be shown at the base of your screen.

Prepare a backup of your Pixel and then restore it to factory settings.

If everything else fails to prevent your Pixel from overheating, a factory reset may be your final resort. If you purchased your phone without any pre-installed apps, this step will uninstall them. To completely erase all of your data, follow this procedure.

To avoid losing any images or sensitive data, back up your smartphone before you begin.

Guide to Using Google Drive for Pixel Backups:

1. Google OneTM may be found on the Google PlayTM Store for download.
2. Adjust the settings.
3. Select Google, and then select Backup.

4. Put in your Google® login credentials when asked.
5. To begin backing up, toggle the Backup by Google One switch to the on position.

A guide to resetting your Pixel to factory settings:

1. Boot up the Settings app on your mobile device.
2. Select System, then Reset options, and finally, Factory Reset to erase all data.
3. Choose Erase all data to remove everything from your phone's internal memory. At times, your phone may prompt you to enter your PIN. Press the "Erase all data" button after entering your PIN.
4. Select "Restart" after your phone's reset is complete.
5. After you've backed up your data, set up your phone.

RESOLVING THE ISSUE OF UNABLE TO PAIR OR DISCONNECT FROM BLUETOOTH

Methods for Resolving the Issue of Unable to Pair or Disconnect from Bluetooth on the Pixel 8 and 8 Pro

Your expectations regarding the software, hardware, and buttery smooth performance of your new

Google Pixel 8 or Pixel 8 Pro were probably rather high when you bought it. Google still has room to improve its software, despite the fact that their premium smartphones excel in many other areas.

The Google Pixel 8 and Pixel 8 Pro have been plagued by problems including overheating, short battery life, and non-functioning Wi-Fi. On top of everything else, users are also complaining about Bluetooth issues with the devices. A lot of people who have the Pixel 8 are having trouble pairing it with their car's Bluetooth. Some impacted users have reported that their Google Pixel would not pair or would repeatedly disconnect.

There are a lot of devices all around us, and the majority of them link to other devices or smartphones over Bluetooth. You probably want to find a solution to the problem of your Google Pixel not being able to connect to a Bluetooth device as soon as possible since it may be a frustrating experience. Luckily, if your Google Pixel 8 or Pixel 8 Pro is experiencing Bluetooth problems, there are a number of viable solutions. Below, I have written them down.

Have you ever had problems with the Google Pixel 8 or 8 Pro's Bluetooth connection? Issues Resolved

You have probably already tried powering off and then turning on Bluetooth as a possible issue before we get to the answers. If you haven't done so before, enter the quick settings panel by swiping down from the top of your screen. Then, touch on the Bluetooth icon. After you've turned it on by tapping the symbol again, you may attempt to link your Pixel to your vehicle or another device.

I have more alternatives listed below in case turning Bluetooth off and on doesn't solve the problem.

Restart your pixel device

Reboot A broken Bluetooth connection might be the result of an issue with your Google Pixel's software. Rebooting the device usually fixes the problem. You may also force your device to reconnect to associated devices by restarting it, which refreshes the Bluetooth connection.

If you own a Pixel 8 or Pro, you may restart it by pressing the power button together with the volume-up button. Establish a Bluetooth connection with your second device after it has finished booting up. Remember that Bluetooth only works over a limited range. Consequently, for a successful connection, your phone has to be close to the other device.

Reboot the Pixel

Your Google Pixel will attempt to connect to the most recently connected device when you activate Bluetooth. It may not attempt to connect to every associated device immediately. Turning on Bluetooth may, however, not be sufficient. To connect a device, open Bluetooth settings and then touch on the device you want to link.

Next, use the other device's mobile data pixel wifi quick settings to see if it is currently communicating over Bluetooth.

Verify the Bluetooth status on other devices

Both devices must have Bluetooth turned on for the connection to work. At times, we may find that we haven't activated Bluetooth on the other device, even if we've made every effort to connect our phone to it (a vehicle, a speaker, etc.). Verify that you aren't making this dumb error by looking at your other device's Bluetooth status.

To see if it helps, try disabling and then reenabling Bluetooth on the other device. After that, attempt to make a connection by bringing your phone closer.

unpair your Bluetooth devices to remove ads.

If you're experiencing connectivity troubles, pairing failures, or frequent disconnections when using Bluetooth, try removing and repairing your devices. A reliable Bluetooth connection may be restored by following these steps.

This is the whole process:

1. On your Google Pixel, open the Settings app.
2. Press on the Item(s) that are linked. Interconnected gadgets Wireless Bluetooth for Pixel

3. Please select Look at Everything to see all of your Bluetooth devices that are currently connected.
4. Choose Forget by tapping the gear icon that appears next to a device's name.
5. To unpair the device, click the "Forget device" button on the pop-up.
6. To unpair all of your Bluetooth devices, just repeat the process from the beginning.
7. Return to the screen that displays the Connected Devices.
8. To connect to a new device, tap on Bluetooth. [Check that the other device is in pairing mode and has Bluetooth enabled.]

9. Press the name of your device. Finding other Bluetooth devices in the area could take some time.
10. Tap on Pair.

Your other devices should have linked without a hitch, therefore the Bluetooth problems should be over now. After you've tried the above solutions without success, try erasing the Bluetooth cache.

Empty the Bluetooth Cache.

To repair most Bluetooth difficulties, including the ones you're presently experiencing on your Google Pixel 8 or Pixel 8 Pro, clearing the Bluetooth cache is another viable approach. No need to fret! Since this method leaves your linked Bluetooth devices alone, you won't need to pair them again.

The Google Pixel's Bluetooth cache removal process:

1. Get the Settings app started on your mobile device.
2. Find Apps near the bottom of the page and press the button. Your phone's app drawer will be visible to you.
3. To access Bluetooth, locate it in the app list and press the icon.

4. Clear cache may be accessed by tapping on Storage.

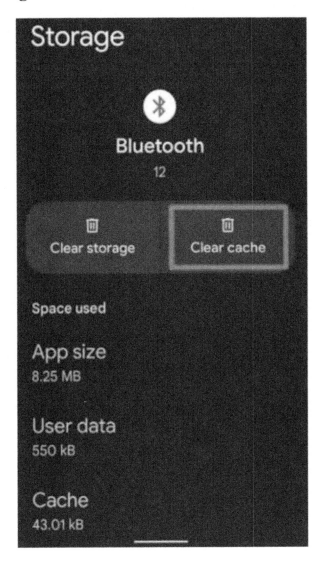

After that, you may see whether the issue persists by trying to pair a Bluetooth device.

Reset Your Network Configuration

When you configure your Google Pixel to utilize Bluetooth, you may encounter issues like connection failure or frequent disconnection if you're not careful. When you reset your network settings, it will erase all of your stored Wi-Fi networks, unpair any Bluetooth devices, and return all of your previously adjusted network settings.

How to Reset Your Pixel's Network Settings:

1. Press on System in the Settings app. Clear All Network Settings on Android

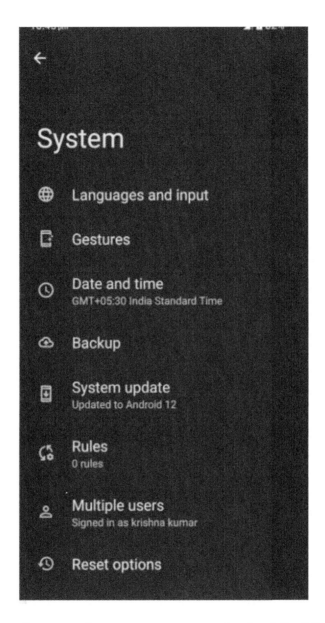

Select the option to reset. Android Network Settings Reset (4)

2. Please choose Reset Wi-Fi, mobile & Bluetooth.

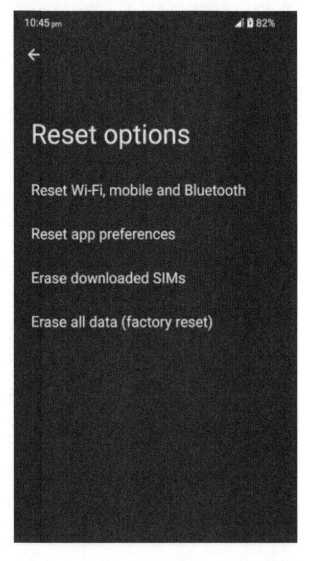

3. To confirm, click on RESET SETTINGS. Go to
   the Settings > Network > Reset app

4. After you've reset your network, you may link your Bluetooth device by going into your phone's Bluetooth settings.

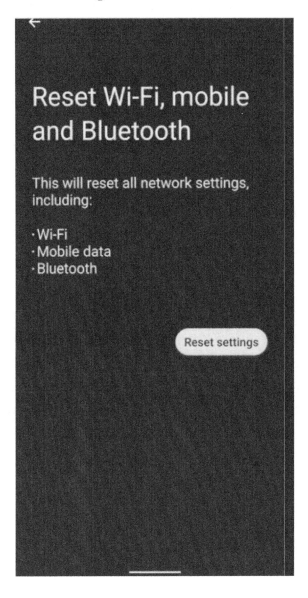

Enter Safe Mode When Turning On Your Google Pixel

The Bluetooth issues you're experiencing can be caused by third-party programs on your smartphone. Boot your smartphone into safe mode to check for any dangerous applications.

All third-party applications will be temporarily disabled when your smartphone enters safe mode. Therefore, a problematic app on your Google Pixel is to blame if Bluetooth is functional and can connect to other devices in safe mode.

Steps to enter safe mode after starting a Google Pixel:

1. When prompted, press and hold the power button in addition to the volume up button to access the power menu.
2. Once the opportunity to reboot to safe mode displays, tap and hold the Restart option until it disappears.
3. Press OK to verify. After entering safe mode, the device should restart.

The phrase "Safe mode" will appear in the bottom left corner of your screen while you are in safe mode. Please try pairing your Google Pixel with another Bluetooth device to see if it resolves the issue.

To identify the source of Bluetooth problems when in safe mode, quit the mode and remove each newly installed app one by one. Turning off safe mode is as simple as restarting your device.

Enhance Your Device

HOW TO TROUBLESHOOT RECEIVING MESSAGES

Using an eSIM on a Google Pixel 8 Pro and Not Receiving Messages

There may be an issue if you have used a physical SIM on a prior phone and are now using an eSIM on your Google Pixel 8 Pro.

If you were previously using the physical SIM on your old phone and are now using the T-Mobile services eSIM on your Google Pixel 8 Pro, for instance, you will need to make certain adjustments in order for your Pixel 8 Pro to receive text messages.

Turn off the Real Time Messaging feature on your previous phone.

Force restarts the Pixel 8 Pro.

- To activate RCS conversations on your Pixel 8 Pro, open the "Messages" app and go to "Settings->RCS chats." activate the feature.

- The use of RCS chat
- The next step is to confirm your phone number; after that, you'll see "Status: Connected" in the upper right corner of the RCS chat window.
- Confirm the RCS talk

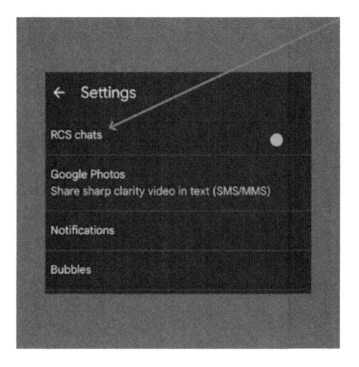

To deactivate RCS chat on the prior device, follow these steps if you don't have it with you.

If you used to use an iPhone but now use an Android, you need to disable your number from iMessage.

- You may now get verification codes and SMS messages on your Google Pixel 8 Pro. Ignoring the problem with text messages won't help, so you'll need to clear your phone's cache.

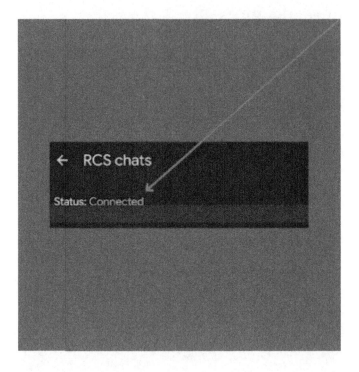

Empty the Messages App's Cache and Delete Any Saved Data

1. Locate "Settings" on your mobile device.
2. To go to "Apps->See All Apps" and then to "Messages."
3. Go to the "Storage & cache" menu, and from there, choose "Clear cache" or "Clear Storage."

Erasing Cache Folder

Process for erasing data from a cache partition

Erase message app cache

1. Turn off your phone.
2. When the "Fastboot Mode" screen displays, press and hold the "Power" and "Volume" buttons simultaneously.
3. Finally, press the power button to finalize your selection after using the volume buttons to navigate the menu.

4. After that, choose "recovery mode," and then press and hold the "Volume UP" and "Power" keys simultaneously while the "no command" label shows on the screen.
5. Utilize the Volume buttons and power button to confirm the choice "Wipe Cache partition" when in recovery mode.
6. After everything is finished, choose "Reboot the System Now" to reboot your phone.

Revamp the Phone's App

Verify whether your phone has received any new patches recently. Fixes for bugs and enhancements to specific features are common in patch updates.

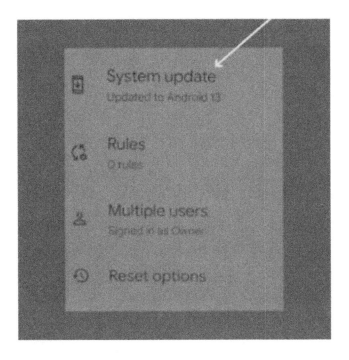

1. In updating the Google Pixel software, access the phone's "Settings" menu.
2. Go to the "System" menu and open the "System update".
3. You'll see instructions for downloading and installing the updates. Just follow them.

GOOGLE PIXEL APPS NOT WORKING?

The user experience of Pixel 6 customers has been plagued by annoying app crashes. Many consumers are perplexed as to why and how to repair the frequent app crashes on Google's newest flagship phone. Here, we'll examine the most common causes of app crashes on Pixel 6 smartphones and provide practical solutions that users may use to fix these issues.

One option is to restart the Pixel.

When troubleshooting a phone, the first thing to do is restart the device. To reset your phone and fix any memory problems, just turn it off and then turn it back on again. To check whether the crashes have persisted after restarting, open the applications. Bring your Pixel 6 or Pixel 6 Pro back to life by:

- For a few seconds, keep pressing the power button.

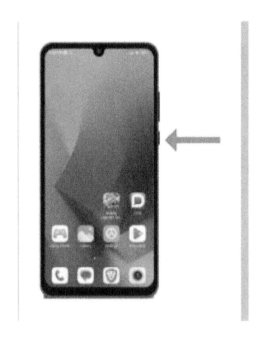

- Press "Restart" when asked to do so.

Recheck for Updates to Your System and Apps

App crashes may be caused by out-of-date software, so make sure your Pixel 6 is completely updated:

- Open System in the Settings menu, then System Update.
- Apply any new operating system patches.
- Just launch the Play Store app.
- Select "Profile" from the menu. Oversee software and hardware > Updating information is now accessible
- Stay up-to-date with all the latest app updates.

Make sure crashes aren't caused by a patched bug by updating your system software and applications.

Disable App Battery Optimization

On occasion, the Pixel 6's battery efficiency function could be too tight in its limiting of background app resources. If an app keeps crashing, you may disable battery optimization:

Navigate to the Settings menu, then choose Apps. Then, find the 3 on 10 jpg file.

- Choose the program

- Select "Battery" then "Battery optimization." Avoid maximizing
- The app should operate without any hiccups when battery optimization is turned off.

Clear Cache Partition

If the program is crashing due to corrupt files, clearing the cache partition might fix the problem. Clearing the cache partition:

- Put your Pixel 6 to sleep.

- To access the boot menu, press and hold the power button and the volume down button simultaneously.
- To choose "Wipe cache partition," press and hold the volume buttons.
- To choose it, press the Power button.
- In the end, you'll see "Cache wipe complete."
- Hit the "Reboot system now" button.

Apps shouldn't crash at random anymore after clearing the cache.

Remove New Versions of Apps

Uninstalling the update could resolve app crashes that occurred after it:

- Launch the Play Store and then touch the profile picture.

- Select Manage Apps and Devices. Peruse all available programmes
- To remove updates, open the app and tap on it.

You can get the program back to a stable version where it doesn't crash by uninstalling the newest update.

Enter Safe Mode upon Boot

To ensure that no third-party applications are to blame for any problems, safe mode loads just the most necessary apps and services:

- Keep holding down the Power button
- Continue pressing the "Power off" button for a while.

251

- Select "OK" to proceed with the safe mode reboot.

Crashing when in safe mode indicates that an external program is probably to blame. Remove or update programs that you have installed lately.

Clear All Your App Data

To remove faulty settings that may be causing problems, you may reset the app's preferences:

- To see all applications, go to Settings > Applications.
- Scroll down to "More options" and press the ">" button. Delete all saved app data

If you're experiencing crashes, try resetting your preferences. This will return programs to their original start settings.

Raise an issue with Google's support team.

Contact Google Support if you have exhausted all troubleshooting methods and your applications continue to break unexpectedly:

- Use the Settings app on your Pixel phone to have a live conversation with a Google representative.

- For assistance, post in the Pixel Phone Help thread and Google employees will respond.
- If you're having trouble repairing problems on your Pixel 6, call Google support and talk with an agent.
- Google is able to provide extra diagnostic information and software repair suggestions for the crashing situation by analyzing debug logs.

Reset the Pixel to Factory Settings .

If all else fails, you may always do a factory reset to erase all data and return your phone to its original settings. If the crash is caused by software, a factory reset will fix it. Once the reset is finished, you may restore your applications and data. Always back up your data before:

Find "System" in the Settings menu, then "Reset options." Factory reset to erase all data

- Click on the "Reset phone" option.
- Select Remove All Data.
- Resetting Your Google Pixel to Factory Settings

At some time, most Google Pixel owners will likely do a factory reset. There are a few differences between resetting a Pixel and other Android smartphones that can throw you off. You should still familiarize yourself with the safe methods of doing a factory reset, regardless of whether you have just purchased the flagship Pixel 8 or the new Pixel 7a. In this tutorial, you will learn how to successfully do a factory reset as well as what occurs thereafter.

CHAPTER ELEVEN

HOW TO RESTORE TO FACTORY SETTINGS

My Google Pixel has been restored to factory settings; what now?

If you want to return your phone to its original factory settings and remove all data, you may do a factory reset. Anything from images and videos to contacts and files to applications and conversations to passwords and more falls under this category. Before you conduct a factory reset on your Pixel, whether you're trying to fix an issue or trade it in, make sure you back up all of your data. This is because data saved in the cloud may be recovered.

Things to remember before resetting your Google Pixel to factory settings

Before you can safely do a factory reset, be sure you follow these steps:

- The login credentials for the phone's Google Account are known to you.
- Password, pattern, or PIN, you know it all with this phone.
- You saved a copy of your files to your Google Drive.

- The phone is now charging while plugged in.

Before you start using Google Authenticator, make sure to export your account.

Resetting Your Google Pixel to Factory Settings

To restore your Google Pixel to its factory settings, take these steps:

1. Start up the Settings app.
2. Tap System after scrolling to the bottom.

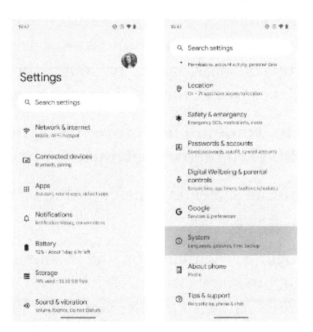

Get into your Pixel's Settings.

3. On your Google Pixel phone, go to System.
4. Select Reset settings from the System menu that appears.

5. For a factory reset, choose Erase all data. Prior to doing a factory reset, try the various reset options available while troubleshooting your phone.
6. To reset your Pixel smartphone, press the Reset button.
7. To do a factory reset on your Pixel smartphone, choose Erase all data.

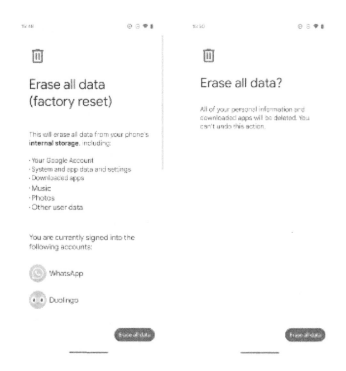

Press the "Erase all data" button located in the screen's bottom right corner. The accounts that you have logged into are shown on this screen. Verify that you have a backup copy of the login information for each.

1. To access your phone, input its passcode, pattern, or PIN.
2. To initiate the factory reset, tap the "Erase all data" button located in the bottom right corner of your screen. Once you take this step, there's no turning back.

3. Prior to wiping all data, make sure you have checked all the accounts that are associated with your Pixel.
4. Choose "Erase all data" to finish wiping your Pixel.

Rest assured, a factory reset might take a few minutes. After the factory reset is finished, your phone will restart and show you the setup screen from when you first set it up. Verify that you can install Android 14 if you were using an earlier version of the operating system.

The new Pixel allows you to do more.

Your phone is ready for use or shipping after a factory reset. To make some money while doing your bit for the environment, consider donating or trading in your old phone instead of engaging in a trade-in program or giving away your gadget.

METHODS FOR BOOTING INTO AND OUT OF SAFE MODE

Perhaps you purchased a Google Pixel 4 or 4 XL in 2019. But there's a chance that the phone may start acting up later on. A program you installed not long ago might be to blame. If that's the case, the Pixel 4's safe mode should fix the issue.

Could you please explain what "safe mode" is? This option essentially restricts app execution to just those from the official app store. This would indicate that a third-party software was responsible if your issue disappeared when using this option.

Here are two ways to put your Pixel phone into safe mode that we've compiled for your convenience. The instructions for leaving safe mode will also be provided to you.

Methods for booting into safe mode on the Pixel

1. Keep the power button pressed down until the power off symbol appears.
2. Hold down the Power Off symbol until the Safe Mode icon appears.
3. The Pixel 4 may enter Safe Mode by tapping the corresponding icon.
4. After a few seconds, the phone should power back on, and a safe mode indication should appear in the screen's lower left corner.
5. Once you've resolved the issue with your phone, just press and hold the Power button once again to restart it in regular mode.

For Pixel 4 phones, this is the procedure to follow in order to enter Safe Mode after the device is turned off:

1. To power on, press and hold the button. By now, you should feel a vibration and be able to see the phone's logo on the screen.
2. Hold down the left side of the phone's volume down button while releasing the power button; this should be done while the "logo screen" is still showing.
3. Hold down the volume down button until you reach the home screen. On the bottom left corner of the screen, you should notice the Safe mode indicator.
4. Once you've resolved the issue with your phone, just press and hold the Power button once again to restart it in regular mode.

Exit strategies

The quickest way to get out of safe mode on a Pixel 4 is this:

1. To access your phone's settings, press and hold the Power button until a menu appears.
2. Crank up the reboot machine. Keep pressing the Power button for another 30 seconds if you still don't see a restart option.

If this doesn't work, here's another way to get out of safe mode:

1. Switch off your Google Pixel 4 device.
2. Hold down the Power button until your gadget turns off.
3. Release the Power button once the logo appears on the screen.
4. Hold down the Volume Down button for a few seconds after you release the Power button.

Here you can find the steps to enter and leave safe mode on Pixel 4 phones. Post a comment and tell us if you know of any additional ways to enter or leave these modes.

METHODS FOR FACTORY RESETTING THE GOOGLE PIXEL 8 PRO'S CELLULAR DATA SETTINGS

Slow data speeds, lost calls, or an inability to connect to a cellular network? If you're encountering any of these problems, resetting your mobile network settings can be a good first step in troubleshooting.

If you want to keep your stored Wi-Fi networks and passwords, you'll have to type them all in again after this. Furthermore, after the reset is finished, your phone can restart itself.

Prior to Starting

Get the name and password for your Wi-Fi network ready before you go ahead and do anything. As an additional security safeguard, you should back up your phone's data in a secure place.

Procedure for Clearing Mobile Network Settings

1. Go to Settings: The Settings app may be found and tapped on your Google Pixel 8 Pro.
2. Go to the System menu: Locate the "System" option by swiping down in the Settings menu.
3. Go to the System menu, then look for the "Reset options" tab and press on it.

Start up the Preferences and select System. Navigate to the Reset menu.

> Access the reset options under Settings > System.

4. Set Up Your Mobile Network Select "Reset Mobile Network Settings" to reset your network settings.
5. Confirm the reset by seeing a confirmation screen. Press the "Reset settings" button to continue.
6. Verify the Reset by Entering PIN or Password: If asked, enter the PIN or password for your phone.

7. Complete Reset: To confirm and complete the reset of the network settings, touch "Reset settings" again.

Choose the option to Reset Mobile Network Settings, Select the option to Reset Settings. Just plug in your security lock. Press the Reset settings button to begin.

Before you may reset your mobile network's settings, you must go to the settings menu.

The settings for your mobile network have been reset. You may have to manually restart your phone, or it could restart itself. To go back online once your phone has rebooted, enter the name and password of your Wi-Fi network again.

Extra Tips for Fixing the Problem

Here are some things to try if you still have problems connecting to your mobile network after restarting your device:

1. Install Any Available Software Updates: Make sure your Pixel 8 Pro has all the latest software updates installed. Fixes for bugs and improvements to performance are common components of updates.
2. Please restart your phone. If you're experiencing intermittent problems with your network connection, try restarting your device.
3. Switching Mobile Data: You could see if it helps to toggle your mobile data connection on and off. In rare cases, this may fix short-lived connectivity issues.
4. If you continue to have problems, it is advisable to reach out to your cellular provider for assistance. They may be able to help you with further troubleshooting steps or spot issues that might be connected to your account.

If you're having problems connecting to the internet on your Google Pixel 8 Pro, try resetting your mobile network settings by following these instructions and taking other troubleshooting advice into account.

HOW TO CLEAR THE GOOGLE PIXEL CACHE SPACE

Following these easy instructions will allow you to delete the cache disk on your Google Pixel 6. You should educate yourself about the cache before you begin clearing it. A Google Pixel Six's cache is its internal storage. It will make your surfing experience faster, but it will slow down your Google Pixel 6 as it consumes up storage space. You may think of the cache as a navigational memory. The cache will save a variety of information, including your browser history, a website's graphic data, and application data. You may clear the cache using a few methods. There are steps that you may follow here.

Get Rid of Google Pixel 6's Cache

Emptying your Android device's cache on a regular basis can help you minimize the storage on your Google Pixel 6. Here are some things you can do to fix it.

Clear cache and partition.

1. On your Google Pixel 6, go to the Settings menu.
2. To delete cached data, go to Preferences > Warehouse > Cache Data.
3. To clean, go to Parameter > Warehouse > Cleaner.
4. Remove All App Data from Your Google Pixel 6's Cache

If you own an Android device, you may clear the app's cache in a few different methods.

1. Here are the methods for those of you who choose to clear your Google Chrome browser cache:

- Launch a web browser.
- Tap the three dots in the upper right corner of your screen.
- Locate your device's settings and click on them.
- Select the option for private safety.
- A clean browsing history is an option you must choose.

2. Finally, click on "Clear 2" after verifying. You may follow this guide to erase your cache while in recovery mode:
   - Press and hold both the power and volume buttons simultaneously.
   - When you hear your phone vibrating, let go of the volume button.
   - Press the power button after searching for "Wipe Cache Partition."
   - Press the power button to confirm.
   - Finally, choose the Reboot system now option.

Justifications for Consistently Cleaning Cache

Your most-visited website will be easier to reach when you neglect to clear your cache. You may avoid typing the address of the website twice, which saves you time. Typically, your browser will delete temporary files from your device. Your hard drive's space could be filled up if you don't clear your cache often. Your device's performance can degrade as it fills up your hard disk. Clearing your cache is necessary for other reasons as well.

1. Some problems can be easily solved.
2. Because of malware, you should clear your cache. Your device might be put at risk if any caches contain malware.
3. To restore lost storage space on your Google Pixel 6, clearing your cache is a must.

Clearing the cache on your Google Pixel 6 is a breeze if you follow the instructions above. Since you'll have more room on your smartphone, you can multitask much more quickly. The Google Pixel 6 cache partition erase process may now begin.

Printed in Great Britain
by Amazon

42903271R00155